Cultivating Christian Community

Thomas R. Hawkins

DISCIPLESHIP RESOURCES

PO BOX 340003 • NASHVILLE, TN 37203-0003
www.discipleshipresources.org

To the people of
Johnstown and Lerna United Methodist Churches
and Loxa Presbyterian Church

Reprinted 2004.

Cover and book design by Joey McNair

Edited by Debra D. Smith and Cindy S. Harris

ISBN 0-88177-327-1

Library of Congress Catalog Card No. 00-105426

Scripture quotations, unless otherwise indicated, are from the New Revised Standard Version of the Bible, copyright © 1989 by the Division of Christian Education of the National Council of the Churches of Christ in the USA. All rights reserved. Used by permission.

DR327

Table of Contents

Chapter One

Community:
God's Gracious Gift

H ow very good and pleasant it is when kindred live together in unity!"
exclaims the psalmist (Psalm 133:1). Living in community as God's
people is the goal and fulfillment of human life. It is the precondition
for human life itself. There is no *I* apart from *we*. Human life cannot exist
apart from relationships in community. Deprived of community, we experience a cavernous sense of meaninglessness, an aching void that haunts many
modern lives.

Sally and Jim live in the outermost suburb of a major city. Jim wakes long
before dawn, swings past the drive-through window to pick up coffee and a
roll, and fights his way to work on the expressway. Jim eats lunch alone in a
fast-food restaurant around the corner from his office. In the evenings and on
weekends, Jim is usually too exhausted from his long commute to interact with
friends or family. He knows none of his neighbors. He has no time for community or school involvement. He barely has time for Sally and their two sons.
Jim feels isolated from his family, his coworkers, and his neighbors. Beyond
his physical weariness, Jim wonders if his life has any center, any meaning, any
connection to a larger vision and purpose.

Marian has seen many changes in her small rural community. She
remembers when her mile-long road was home to seven other farm families.
All of them have sold out and left. Many of her friends have died or relocated

to be near their adult children. Marian's own sons and daughters have moved to distant cities where they can find employment. She finds herself increasingly isolated and alone. Time and economic changes have erased the community that once embraced her. She worries about what might happen if she falls and breaks her hip. She wonders, *How long will I lie here before someone finds me?*

Like Jim, Sally, and Marian, all of us are touched by the loneliness and isolation that accompany the absence of community. We yearn for a feeling of connection and relationship. Corporate interests constantly exploit this longing. They promise that we can be connected to the whole world if we only purchase their technology or buy their products. Yet community requires more than the newest technologies or the latest digitized communication. We restlessly search for a communion that heals our hearts and renews our spirits.

There Is No Life Apart From Community

Nothing in all creation exists apart from community. At the most basic physical level, all forms of matter seek relationship, connection, and communion. Subatomic particles are attracted to other particles. Microbes combine into larger organisms. Galaxies emerge from primordial swirling gas clouds into coherent shapes.

What is true for atoms and microbes is true for us. People grow and find nourishment through the giving and returning of attention and recognition. This flow of care and concern moves from us to others and from others to us. When this rhythm breaks, our lives are broken by alienation and separation. When others fail to acknowledge and recognize us, we feel cut off and alone. Experiences of communion, on the other hand, bridge the spaces that divide us. The need to be known, to have our experience understood and accepted by another, is meat and drink to the human heart.

Life is the gift of community. There is no life that is not life in community. Our lives are gifts that come to us from relationships in community. Nothing is more personal and intimate than our names. Yet we do not name ourselves. We receive our names in the midst of a community that names and claims us. A pastor holds us, pours water on our foreheads, and says, "Mary, I baptize you."

If we trace our "natural talents" back to their ultimate source, we discover communities of neighbors, family, mentors, friends, or teachers. None of us are self-made creatures. We are constituted through the communities that have embraced us, loved us, and nurtured us.

There Is No *I* Apart From *We*

Our lives are constituted and sustained by relationships in community. Without these relationships, we cease to be human.

Franz Kafka's fable "The Metamorphosis" describes a young traveling salesman who lives a lonely, isolated life. He takes public transportation to work without speaking to those sitting next to him. He retires to his room each evening without making contact with his family. One morning he wakes to discover that he has become a cockroach. His frightened family deprives him of all the ways in which we recognize one another as fellow humans. They lock him in his room. They remove the furniture, obliterating all signs of human community. They throw food scraps onto the floor rather than share a meal with him. In the end, he dies alone and no longer human.

Kafka's fable reminds us that we are only human when we live in community. We live by the recognition we extend to and receive from one another. When we are deprived of this recognition, we cease to be human.

I once volunteered to ring the Salvation Army bell outside a post office during the holidays. I was amazed at how invisible I became to customers going in and out for their Saturday mail. I was wearing a bright red coat and a funny red hat. Yet most customers refused to make eye contact with me. No one would greet me. I would say, "Good Morning!" or, "Merry Christmas!" and they would rush swiftly through the door without saying a word. To acknowledge me would require them to acknowledge the human needs that my ringing bell and clanging bucket represented. Their refusal to recognize me rendered me invisible. Their eyes did not see me. I felt somehow unreal. I ceased to exist both in their eyes and my own.

As we pass homeless people on the street, our eyes carefully avoid contact with their eyes. We deny them recognition as people worthy of our attention. We meet people sitting in wheelchairs as we step into the elevator. We quietly keep our eyes on our shoes. We refuse to acknowledge them as human beings who deserve our concern or regard.

A person with a disability once told me that her greatest suffering is not the physical condition with which she was born. It is the psychological and spiritual pain of constantly being treated as invisible, as a nonentity, as someone less than human. Another friend explained to me that he smiles and speaks whenever he passes a young, black male on the streets. Our society as a whole has rendered such young men invisible. His smile is a deliberate act of recognition and inclusion.

God has created people for community. Only within community is authentic humanity possible. There is no life that is not lived in community. "It is not good that the man should be alone" (Genesis 2:18). So God creates us to be partners in a common life. We discover our deepest selves when we live face-to-face and side by side with others in the give-and-take of relationship. Before we can speak in the singular, we learn to speak in the plural. We cannot say *I* without first saying *we*.

The Dilemma of Human Community

Community is the joy and fulfillment of being human; yet it is also our deepest dilemma. We know that our very existence depends upon mutual acknowledgment and recognition. But such recognition cannot be coerced. It comes as a gift. What we most need, we cannot secure for ourselves. When we try to secure it, it eludes our grasp.

Love and fear are at war within us. We love others by granting them the recognition and acknowledgment that include them in a common humanity. We, in turn, rely upon others to bestow their recognition upon us. But we also fear that others will not respond to our need for recognition and acknowledgment. We fear that they will not love us as we have loved them.

This loving or not loving of other people is literally a matter of life and death. So, out of fear, we try to coerce what can only be given as a gift. We attempt to secure for ourselves what comes as grace. We control and clutch at others, commanding them to recognize us because of our achievements and accomplishments. Through boasting, we hope to command others' recognition and acknowledgment (see Romans 3:27; 1 Corinthians 1:27-31; Galatians 6:13-14).

Paul saw the futility of this whole fear-driven project. He described it as sin and death. "For 'no human being will be justified in his sight' by deeds prescribed by the law, for through the law comes the knowledge of sin" (Romans 3:20). Sin is the death of humankind because sin is the breaking up of the communion by which we live. Our attention becomes fixed on getting what we need. We no longer widen the scope of our attention, giving others the loving gaze of relationships-in-community. We no longer view others as worthy for their own sakes of our recognition and inclusion in community. We instead see them as objects useful to us in confirming our own worth and importance. In the process, everyone is deeply wounded. Others fail to recognize us, depriving us of inclusion in loving communion. We then respond by refusing them the recognition they need. Dividing walls of exclusion and hostility emerge between people.

When atoms are split apart, the result is a violent explosion. Nuclear fission is the most powerful source of energy we know. It can incinerate cities and vaporize whole nations. Similarly, when people sin against one another by denying the recognition and relationship basic to human existence, the result is an explosion of violence, rage, and inhumanity.

When, on the other hand, people come together in mutuality and community, God's gifts are released. People experience a sign and foretaste of God's reign. "For where two or three are gathered in my name, I am there among them" (Matthew 18:20).

God's Gracious Initiative in Creating Community

What we cannot achieve on our own, God graciously provides. We do not build or organize community. Community is a grace that breaks into our midst. God initiates community. God graciously reaches out and invites us into a community we cannot establish from our own resources or by our own achievements.

Christians affirm that God is Trinity: One God in Three Persons. God as Trinity reveals a community of love between the Creator, the Christ, and the Spirit. This communion of love overflows and reaches out into all creation, inviting every living creature to join in its endless dance of love and relationship.

Scripture tells the story of God's persistent effort to invite all creatures into communion. God ceaselessly creates community where there is alienation, reconciliation where there is enmity, redemption where there is bondage. This love of God overcomes the fears that prevent us from experiencing community. "Beloved, let us love one another, because love is from God. . . . God is love, and those who abide in love abide in God, and God abides in them. . . . There is no fear in love, but perfect love casts out fear" (1 John 4:7, 16b, 18).

The entire history of Israel testifies to God's initiative in creating community. Immediately after the scattering of people and the confounding of languages at Babel, God called Abraham and Sarah. Abraham and Sarah were invited into a communion with God that was the sign, foretaste, and instrument of a new community. This new community would reverse Babel's alienation. "You will be a blessing. I will bless those who bless you, and the one who curses you I will curse; and in you all the families of the earth shall be blessed" (Genesis 12:2-3).

In the Exodus, God took a mixed gathering of slaves, refugees, and immigrants from bondage to freedom. God transformed those who were *not* a people into *God's* people. Slaves whom the Egyptians had refused to acknowledge as fully human suddenly became full participants with God in creating God's new community.

Once you were not a people,
but now you are God's people;
once you had not received mercy,
but now you have received mercy.

(1 Peter 2:10)

God provides what human will and determination alone cannot accomplish. God creates true community. The people that God calls into community are those who have experienced deliverance from bondage, healing from brokenness, birth from spiritual death, reconciliation from alienation.

The Hebrew Scripture's terms for the community of faith capture this sense of divine initiative and human response. *Qahal* (assembly), *'edah* (congregation), and *sôd* (assembly) all suggest that God gathers the people. God initiates community. We respond with praise and gratitude for God's gracious provision of this basic human need for communion.

Jesus and Community

In Jesus, God creates a community where all sorts and conditions of people find a welcome. God inaugurates a hospitable communion where strangers recognize one another's common humanity and so overcome sin, alienation, and death. Jesus accomplishes our salvation when he establishes the possibility of communion among us.

The reason for Jesus' crucifixion may not lie in what Jesus preached and taught. Many of his sayings and parables were similar to what other rabbis of his time said. What ultimately led to his death were his table manners. Jesus invited the wrong people to the intimacy of table fellowship.

When Jesus acted as a neighbor to sinners and persuaded them to be neighbors in faithfulness each to the other's humanity, he initiated community. In Jesus' table fellowship with sinners and outcasts, he invited into community individuals wounded by a society that refused to acknowledge them as equal partners in a common humanity. Sinners were not just people who were ritually impure. They were people who engaged in activities and occupations that rendered them unacceptable and invisible. Like the homeless men and women on our streets, these sinners were the poorly paid and the exploited. They were people with disabilities. To be a sinner was to be denied the human recognition and community that made one fully human.

Jesus' acts of healing were more than miracles in which he mended broken minds and bodies. Jesus' healings restored people to community. Disease isolates people. It denies them acceptance into community. Even today we stigmatize people who suffer from certain diseases. We refuse to touch them. We closet them away from sight. We deny them recognition as sharing in a common humanity.

The woman with the chronic flow of blood was not just physically troubled. Her blood made her ritually impure. She was excluded from the community of her synagogue. She was cut off from intimate contact with her husband and family. When Jesus healed her, he did not just cure her of a physical limitation. He restored her to participation in human community (Mark 5:25-34). One important goal of Jesus' healings was to help people recover mutuality and communion.

The Cross and Community

Sin is a vicious cycle. We refuse to acknowledge other people because they have refused to acknowledge us. We are indifferent to others because others are indifferent to us. Refusal to love breeds more refusal to love. We sin because we are sinned against. We repeat toward others what we ourselves have experienced.

The miracle of Jesus is that this vicious circle was broken in his life, death, and resurrection. Here was a person who did not respond with indifference even when met with indifference. He did not sin even when sinned against: "Father, forgive them; for they do not know what they are doing" (Luke 23:34). When denied recognition and treated as someone outside the circle of human concern, he continued to treat others with unconditional regard, acknowledging them as his brothers and sisters: "Truly I tell you, today you will be with me in Paradise" (Luke 23:43). When met by coercion and fear, he responded with loving concern: "He said to his mother, 'Woman, here is your son.' Then he said to the disciple, 'Here is your mother'" (John 19:26-27a).

Jesus took the full fury of a humanity that had become less than human because it had known only fear, hostile exclusion, and the refusal of communion. He accepted the hostility of those whose humanity had been violated, forgave them, and thus reestablished the possibility of a common human bond both between himself and them and between them and others. "This is my commandment, that you love one another as I have loved you. No one has greater love than this, to lay down one's life for one's friends" (John 15:12-13).

Jesus broke the vicious circle of sin breeding more sin. He shattered the cycle of indifference breeding more indifference, of the refusal of recognition spawning more hostile refusals. By his actions Jesus overcame the conditions that destroy the possibility of communion among all people. With Jesus' life, death, and resurrection, God takes the initiative in restoring the possibility of genuine community to humankind.

Knowing that our deepest human need is for relationships in community, we frantically seek to build and create a sense of communion. But the community we ultimately need comes not from our own human efforts but as a gift of God's grace. We do not create community. We receive the gift of community and give thanks to the One who makes it possible. There is no life that is not lived in community, and there is no community that does not live in praise and service to God.

Chapter Two

Characteristics of Spiritual Community

S ome people claim that the pace and distractions of modern life have eroded our sense of community. But perhaps it is the other way around. We are distracted and overextended because we have forgotten how to live in communion with God and others. Lacking spiritual community, our lives become uncentered and filled with distractions. They spin faster and faster. They whirl out of control.

Modern life does not undermine the possibility of community; the absence of community creates the frantic distractions and relentless pace of modern life. We live in a culture that values individualism while dismissing the importance of relationships. We act as if we should outgrow our childish need for others in the same way that we outgrew training wheels on our bicycles. We confuse being adult with being separate. We mistake individuality for authenticity. We believe that we can be adult only if we live unencumbered by community, so we abandon the communities of friends and family that weave life into a meaningful whole.

As a result, our society is spiritually starved for community. The frenetic pace and constant distractions of modern life do not cause a decline in spiritual community. Rather, as we cease to anchor our lives in genuine spiritual community, we frantically search for something to fill the void.

Spiritually Starved for Community

The effects of this spiritual starvation are everywhere: anger, violence, escapist behavior, substance abuse, control, and manipulation. The constant expression of anger—from road rage to rudeness in the shopping line—is a sign of our relational emptiness. Escapist behaviors and addictions momentarily fill this emptiness. They give people a false illusion of communion. Some people try to overcome these feelings by controlling others, manipulating them into giving the recognition and acknowledgment they so desperately seek.

Having forgotten how it feels to live in genuine communion with God and others, we seek out pseudo-communities. Some pseudo-communities are built upon rage and anger. They are filled with people united only by their hate and suspicion. Others cater to our addictions but leave our deepest hungers unsatisfied. Some promise power and control, shoring up towers of defense against a threatening world.

We long for the bread of life, but these pseudo-communities offer us the stones of busyness. We seek a place where we can drink deeply the living water of communion; they invite us to entertaining programs designed to satisfy consumer tastes. We come searching for Christian community; they give us service on a committee.

Surrounded by pseudo-communities, how do we recognize genuine spiritual communion? Having been taught that we should grow beyond the need for community in the same way we outgrew our childhood toys, how do we identify Christian community when we experience it?

What Is Spiritual Community?

Historically, the church's creeds have used four basic dimensions to identify true Christian community. When we pray the Nicene Creed, we profess our belief in "one holy catholic and apostolic church."[1] These four dimensions of the church—one, holy, catholic, and apostolic—suggest at least six basic qualities by which we can recognize genuine spiritual community in Christ:

1. Christian community practices hospitality, creating a safe space where different people feel welcomed, affirmed, visible, and valuable.
2. Christian community is centered on Christ. We share a common focus of relationship in Christ.
3. Christian community practices the means of grace.
4. Christian community occurs when we find healing and wholeness.
5. Christian community invites us to discover our unique gifts for ministry.
6. Christian community equips us to live out our baptismal covenant, sharing in God's work of healing and restoring all creation.

Practicing Hospitality

We experience the oneness of the church when Christian communities offer hospitality. The church's oneness becomes real when people feel welcomed, acknowledged, and recognized as sharing a common humanity in Christ. Christian community creates a safe space where all feel welcomed and included. In Christ we are no longer Greek or Jew, male or female, slave or free. We are one in Christ Jesus (Galatians 3:28). The oneness of the church is experienced in the fellowship of people who are themselves different yet joined together into one body of Christ. The Christian community's oneness lives in a spirit of mutual acceptance (Romans 15:7). People from different social, cultural, and ethnic backgrounds become friends who maintain a oneness of Spirit in the bond of peace (Ephesians 4:3).

"Who would have thought that the first person to use our new ramp would be a child and not one of our older members?" exclaimed Betsy. Betsy's rural congregation had struggled to build a ramp that made their church accessible. Eliminating the uneven, steep steps for older members had been the primary goal. Yet the ramp also made it possible for a new family, whose daughter used a wheelchair, to worship with them. "We feel invisible in so many places because we are excluded," her father explained. "When we saw you constructing a ramp into your building, we knew we would be welcomed here."

Our lives are coauthored with God and others in community. Being recognized and acknowledged is what sustains us as fully human. To be excluded is literally to be sentenced to death. It is to be rendered unreal, invisible, without value. The ugliest word in the English language is the word *exclusivity*. Christian community practices hospitality. A reliable sign of spiritual community is its capacity to create a safe space where all people feel welcomed and included.

Pseudo-communities, on the other hand, require an enemy. They need someone upon whom they can focus their anger and rage. Pseudo-communities exclude some people so that others feel included. Those who seek God only in people who look and act like themselves are apt to find not God but the devil—who will bear an embarrassing resemblance to themselves.

Centered on Christ

The Christian community's catholicity is not a matter of geography or numbers. Its universality is a consequence of its Christ-centeredness. Catholicity refers to our experience of a spiritual community that is centered on Christ, in whom "all the fullness of God was pleased to dwell, and through him God was pleased to reconcile to himself all things, whether on earth or in heaven, by making peace through the blood of his cross" (Colossians 1:19-20).

"A few years ago we had nearly one hundred people worshiping here on

Sundays," Carl said. "But most of those people stopped coming when Pastor Mike left." Congregations sometimes substitute following a charismatic leader for following Christ. Groups become centered upon powerful personalities who use their gifts, talents, or skills to bedazzle others. These leaders use their God-given gifts to put themselves at the center of attention. Pseudo-communities do not have Christ as their center. They replace Christ with someone or something else.

A more subtle form of pseudo-community occurs when we see ourselves as consumers of religious goods and services. Christian community does not then center on Christ. Instead, our needs and wants become the center around which everything revolves. In our addictive culture, people desperately search for a quick fix or for some dazzling entertainment. Pseudo-communities emerge around the meeting of these needs. They offer busyness rather than the bread of life. They substitute activities and programs for faith-forming relationships.

Christian community entails a new focus of relationship in which Jesus Christ, rather than our needs and feelings, is the center. Because this community is centered in Christ rather than in a principle or a program, it is never static and unchanging. It is always in the process of becoming, and this is very difficult. It involves relationships where commitments are broken and people disappointed. Yet Christ always remains the center, graciously forgiving and persistently inviting us to live into the future he makes possible.

Practicing the Means of Grace

Means of grace are practices and spiritual disciplines through which we receive God's grace. Means of grace include acts of compassion and justice as well as traditional spiritual disciplines such as studying the Scripture, public and private worship and prayer, Holy Communion, fasting, and Christian conferencing.

Through practicing the means of grace, congregations encourage people to make Christ the central focus of all relationships. Practicing the means of grace deepens our awareness of how God's sanctifying grace is active in our lives. Through this process of sanctification, we are made holy.

The Nicene Creed uses the word *holy* in two places where Christian community is described. The church is one, holy, catholic, and apostolic. It is also a fellowship of the holy, a communion of saints. Holiness refers to our being sanctified through Christ's activity in us and on us (1 Corinthians 1:2, Colossians 3:12). Christian communities are, therefore, places where we practice the means of grace that guide us toward sanctification.

Leon and Carlos set their alarms an extra hour early on Wednesday mornings. On Wednesdays, they join three other members of their congregation for breakfast. Leon and Carlos are part of a Covenant Discipleship Group. They help each other remain accountable for their practice of spiritual disciplines. Group members tell how they have engaged in acts of personal and corporate piety. Have they prayed? Have they worshiped with others? Have they studied the Scriptures? Have they participated in serving the poor and marginalized? Have they addressed systemic social injustice?

Accountable discipleship groups are one way some Christians practice the means of grace. Spiritual communities are faith-forming communities. They encourage people to practice the means of grace so that their lives may be transformed into a means of grace for the world. We cannot receive the means of grace at the altar if we are not means of grace to and for one another during the week.

Restoring Wholeness

Holiness and wholeness are closely related. Genuine spiritual community therefore restores us to wholeness. Wholeness is a product of love. Where there is love, there is wholeness. It is love that heals and makes whole.

> But he was wounded for our transgressions,
>   crushed for our iniquities;
> upon him was the punishment that made us whole,
>   and by his bruises we are healed.
>
> (Isaiah 53:5)

Wholeness is a heart that does not divide the world into those worthy of compassion and those not worthy of our care and concern. Wholeness—like holiness—is a heart willing to give itself away as Christ gave himself away to make us whole.

In genuine spiritual community, the wounds of failure are embraced and transfigured into the source of our healing. Mistakes and failures are not hidden from sight. They are shared as stimuli to self-examination and learning.

Pseudo-communities, on the other hand, want wholeness without wounds. They confuse being perfect with being made whole. In pseudo-community, mistakes and failures cannot be tolerated. Everything must always be perfect, under control, without error. People in pseudo-communities are emotionally reactive, looking for someone to blame so that their own image of perfection can be maintained.

According to John's Gospel, the risen Christ still bears the wounds of the cross on his hands and side (John 20:19-28). Only the devil appears to be perfect. Evil maintains the pretense of perfection at any price. It is unwilling for any flaw to be revealed. Pseudo-communities promise a perfection that comes without cost, without wounds. They numb and distract. They bolster our pretense of power and control. They leave no room to share our brokenness so that love may heal our wounds and make us whole.

Genuine spiritual community provides a safe space where we can unbind and reveal our wounds, finding healing by opening them to the transforming and transfiguring love of God made known in Jesus Christ. As we share our wounds with Christ and one another, we are restored to wholeness. In some cases, the wounds we reveal are physical. In other cases, these wounds are mistakes, errors, failures that have happened in our relationships and ministries. Spiritual communities are not emotionally reactive. They do not blame and shame. They seek redemptive wholeness, trusting that God can bring new life even from the wreckage of our plans and efforts.

Discovering Our Gifts

Christian community is apostolic because its message is founded upon the witness of the apostles. It is apostolic because the church does not exist for its own sake but for the sake of its mission to and in the world. It is this world that God loves and for which Christ died. It is to this world that we are sent as apostolic ambassadors for Christ (2 Corinthians 5:20). We experience faithful Christian community when we are invited to discover our gifts and are sent forth to employ these gifts in God's world.

"People kept asking me to join our church's prison ministry," Danny began, "but I said prison ministry was not for me. I knew I didn't have the gifts for it. Then my son got into trouble. It was a difficult time for our family. The people in our congregation's prison ministry were there for us. I learned that prison ministry was a lot more than I thought it was. Because of that whole ordeal, I discovered I have something to offer to prisoners and their families. I guess I learned that I should never say never. Our pastor says spiritual gifts are found when our abilities intersect with the world's needs. That's what happened with me and our church's prison ministry."

Pseudo-communities encourage people to become passive consumers of programs and activities. They offer "disabling help"—help that lowers people's confidence in their own abilities, gifts, and strengths. They promote dependency. Christian communities, on the other hand, are communities of gifts and of call. Everyone is encouraged to discover and use their gifts for ministry.

We are called to use our gifts in God's ongoing creative and redemptive activity. As we do so, we fulfill our apostolic mission. Using our gifts for God's ministry is what it means to be the church. One purpose of spiritual community is to help people experience the ways in which they are uniquely gifted, and to help them find outlets for their gifts.

Equipping for Ministry

Christian community is an apostolic community because it equips us to share in God's mission in the world. We encounter genuine community when we are equipped to live out our baptismal covenant. "The gifts he gave were that some would be apostles, some prophets, some evangelists, some pastors and teachers, to equip the saints for the work of ministry, for building up the body of Christ" (Ephesians 4:11-12).

Ministry is not a consumer product provided by religious professionals. We do not consume ministry the way we consume goods and services advertised on storefront windows. We are instead the ones called to ministry. "You are a chosen race, a royal priesthood, a holy nation, God's own people, in order that you may proclaim the mighty acts of him who called you out of darkness into his marvelous light" (1 Peter 2:9). Christian community structures itself around faith-forming opportunities that allow us to experience ourselves as the body of Christ ministering to the world.

Christian communities of faith help us connect faith to faithfulness. If Christians are nestled in a cocoon of religious activities while ignoring the world's suffering, spiritual community is not happening. If Christians are laboring in schools wracked by violence or in offices that make decisions influencing people's lives, but they have no sense that they are engaged in ministry, then Christian community is not present. If pastors have all the power and authority in their congregations so that church members never develop confidence in their own authority as ministers, then genuine community is lacking.

When congregations take seriously the task of equipping the saints for ministry to and in God's world, then every gathering of the church becomes a laboratory for identifying gifts and sharing in ministry. Every meeting, every Bible study, every choir rehearsal is a field of practice where what goes on in the church and what goes on in the world are connected.

Too often congregations separate the content of their gatherings from the long-term goal of equipping people to live out their baptismal covenant in the world. We plan *for* the church's life without trying to *be* the church as we do so. The result is a disparity between how we experience the church's gatherings and the great ends of the church that we espouse. It is as if we gather as a group to play music but never practice our instruments. We simply talk about music theory, learn the history of instruments, and describe great composers from the past.

Congregations that equip people to live out their baptismal covenant make every gathering an opportunity to embody Christian community. Equipping people to live out their baptismal covenant is woven into all aspects of what the church does. Leaders who plan small-group gatherings pay close attention to how their meetings will incarnate God's purpose of spiritual community in Christ. All congregational gatherings ensure that people can discern and share their gifts for ministry. Our small-group settings are a school of practice for those who seek to be disciples.

Where Two or Three Are Gathered

What are these small-group settings where we become disciples of Christ? Small-group settings are a lot like snack foods. They come in all sizes and a wide variety of flavors. Some are sour cream and onion chips. Others are cheese popcorn. Some come in large, family-size boxes. Others are small sacks that fit into a lunch box. Nonetheless, we can cluster most small gatherings into one of five broad categories: accountability groups, support groups, learning groups, service groups, and administrative groups.

Accountability Groups

Early Methodists discovered that mutual accountability was essential for building up discipleship in the world. Developing a sensitivity to how God calls us to be in ministry is a lifetime's task. Learning to follow Christ in our daily lives requires dedication and commitment. It is a discipline that we can sustain only with companions.

Therefore some Christians—like Leon and Carlos—covenant together to watch over one another in love so that each may grow in his or her walk with Christ. Covenant Discipleship Groups are not for interpersonal sharing, though sharing will take place. They are not prayer groups, although members will pray with one another. They are weekly checkpoints for accountability. Covenant Discipleship Groups are not for everyone. They are designed for those who feel God calling them to another level of commitment.

Covenant Discipleship Groups invite Christians to come together and agree upon a group covenant to which they will be mutually accountable. This covenant describes how group members will live out their discipleship in the world. It usually describes acts of personal and corporate piety that will be undertaken: participation in public worship, times of personal prayer, Bible reading, and fasting. It also describes acts of personal and corporate mercy: meeting the needs of individuals and addressing social injustice. Group members use a fixed question-and-answer format in their meetings. The leader asks each member, beginning with himself or herself, whether the intent of each clause of the covenant has been fulfilled during the week. The conversation is thus a controlled dialogue in which the leader asks, advises, reproves, comforts, or exhorts based upon the discipleship covenant.

Accountable discipleship groups are Christ-centered gatherings where people practice the means of grace. They are particularly well suited for equipping Christians to grow in wholeness and to live out their baptismal covenant in the world.

Support Groups

Support groups provide mutual aid or mutual support to their members. Members are usually peers who have common experiences or situations. Many support group meetings are run by and for their members. Members voluntarily participate, seeking mutual support around a common situation or experience.

Donnella still lives in the small town where she grew up. A mother of two small children, Donnella finds being a mother to be confusing and sometimes difficult. Although happily married, Donnella often worries about her husband, who is a recovering alcoholic. Two years ago she read an announcement in her church newsletter about a support group for young mothers. Donnella soon found herself regularly attending these sessions. After a time of Scripture study and prayer, participants talk about their experiences and offer advice. Donnella often leaves feeling that she has received new insights into a problem she is facing. Even when she has nothing to tell the group, Donnella enjoys the other women's warmth and support.

Support groups are Christ-centered small groups where members find healing and wholeness. Support groups create a hospitable environment where participants can be equipped to live out their baptismal covenant.

Learning Groups

Most congregations offer a wide variety of learning settings. These settings range from midweekly Bible studies to Sunday school classes, from short-term Lenten studies to confirmation classes. These gatherings bring together small groups of Christians who wish to learn more about their faith. Some groups may study books of the Bible. Others may examine critical social issues in light of Scripture and tradition.

We have sometimes limited learning groups to formal Christian education programs, but it is time to broaden our definition of how and where learning happens. The term *education* may be more of a hindrance than a help. To some people, education is little more than memorizing facts and dates. To others, education is an expert pouring information into their heads.

Learning groups, however, are ultimately not about facts and information. They are about spiritual development. Learning groups, at their best, foster a deepening awareness of self and a growing engagement with the world. They provide a hospitable space where people can engage in appreciative discovery of their gifts and the world's needs.

Service Groups

These gatherings usually focus on using one's gifts in ministry. Danny's prison ministry story illustrates a typical service group. But service groups need not be solely engaged in ministry outside the church. Choirs and altar guilds, for example, are service groups.

Service groups tend to meet less regularly than learning, support, and accountability groups. They may meet only once a month to share in a particular project. Although members may cherish a sense of belonging and care, such mutuality develops as a byproduct of a more basic interest in an issue or ministry.

Ideally, service groups take time to reflect on the theological or biblical dimensions of their experiences. They link faith with faithfulness, for the One who is the Word is also the Way, and ultimately the Bible is not just Scripture but script. It is not only a text to be read but also a text to be performed in our daily lives.

Gabriella begins weekly choir practice with a short Bible study. The Bible passage connects in some way to the coming Sunday's anthem. Gabriella invites choir members to reflect together on this text. She thus encourages a deepening of choir members' spiritual lives as well as a more effective music ministry. By linking dialogue and reflection with actual service, Gabriella ensures that the work of ministry does not become an end in itself. She sets the choir's service firmly within a process that opens members to larger issues and deeper personal energies. She shapes choir members for ministry through ministry.

Administrative Groups

We gather in small groups for purposes of administration when we meet as a church council, a board of trustees, or a mission committee. These gatherings often provide leadership to the congregation across a wide range of issues and concerns. Administrative groups engage in problem solving, governing, or goal-setting. Donna Markham, in her book *Spiritlinking Leadership*, uses the word *spiritlinking* to describe the work of these small groups.[2] Spiritlinking involves networking and community formation in order to bridge disunity, to make meaning, and to give form to new expressions of God's mission.

The challenge for many congregations is to move away from traditional committee structures that focus on programs and activities. Spiritlinking leadership focuses instead on the fostering of faith-forming relationships.

Terry begins every trustee meeting with a question that helps board members set their work into a larger context. On the evening they discussed the insurance company's report on the church's fire and safety hazards, Terry asked the trustees to discuss this question: When in your life have you looked at your behavior or opinions and changed what you were doing or thinking? The inspection report was then set in a wider context. The task of discussing the insurance inspection became not an end in itself but a means that opened trustees to larger questions and purposes.

For Further Reflection

Take inventory of your congregation's small groups. Using the directions below and the chart on page 24, reflect on how the small groups in your congregation gather as Christian community.

1. List in column one all the small-group gatherings in your congregation.
2. Write in column two what type of group each small group is.
3. Describe in column three each group's participants.
4. Name in column four the resources and tools each group needs to fulfill its purpose.
5. State briefly in column five how the six characteristics of spiritual community (page 14) are or are not present in each group.
6. Discuss the following:
   a. What does this information tell us about our congregation?
   b. What small groups need additional attention or support? Where are the gaps? Where are the centers of energy?
   c. Where are we on the continuum between an activities-centered congregation and a faith-forming community? Why?
   d. How might we weave a spider web of faith-forming relationships that link together the various times, places, and ways we gather as small groups?
   e. What next steps are needed for our small-group gatherings to more fully experience the gift of Christian community?

Endnotes

1 From *The United Methodist Hymnal* (The United Methodist Publishing House, 1989); 880. English translation by the English Language Liturgical Consultation.

2 See *Spiritlinking Leadership: Working Through Resistance to Organizational Change*, by Donna J. Markham (Paulist Press, 1999).

Small Group	Type	Participants	Tools & Resources	Characteristics of Spiritual Community

Chapter Three
The Practice of Community

C hristian community is a gift. It is announced in Jesus' life, death, and resurrection. Jesus breaks the vicious cycle of rejection breeding more rejection, of indifference being met with indifference. He establishes a new community in his body where our common bonds as God's creation may be acknowledged and affirmed.

"For he is our peace; in his flesh he has made both groups into one and has broken down the dividing wall, that is, the hostility between us. . . . So then you are no longer strangers and aliens, but you are citizens with the saints and also members of the household of God" (Ephesians 2:14, 19).

Christian community is not an accident of history. It expresses God's millennia-long purpose to form an abiding and blessed communion among all creation. Christian communities of faith are gatherings of people who have responded to God's gracious gift of community and devote themselves to God's ongoing struggle to restore all creation to this blessed communion.

Discipleship and Community

Community is an already-present reality. Our choice is whether we will gratefully and joyously receive it. Jesus tells two parables about recognizing and receiving an unexpected treasure (Matthew 13:44-46). The farmer did not find the treasure by grim determination and ceaseless effort. Rather, he discovered something hidden all along beneath his very feet. Rejoicing, he responded by selling everything for the sake of this treasure. God's new community is already among us. When we finally recognize it, we are overwhelmed by what we have found. This discovery is so breathtaking that it transforms our lives. "Then in his joy he goes and sells all that he has and buys that field" (Matthew 13:44).

By accepting Jesus' invitation, we abandon our fear-driven habits of enmity, control, and exclusion. We accept God's gift of communion and live in ways that make this community present and visible to others. Our spiritual communities are a sign, foretaste, and instrument of God's new communion in Christ.

Following Jesus means living as if the community he initiated is a gift already present whenever and wherever two or three are gathered together. Discipleship involves pointing with eager expectancy to this gracious community so that all creation may joyfully enter and share its blessings. To be a disciple of Jesus means inviting others to look with the eyes of faith so that they too see this already present community and reorder their lives in response to its presence. "As God's chosen ones, holy and beloved, clothe yourselves with compassion, kindness, humility, meekness, and patience. Bear with one another . . . and whatever you do, in word or deed, do everything in the name of the Lord Jesus, giving thanks to God the Father through him" (Colossians 3:12-13, 17).

This community is present when we gather as the church of Jesus Christ. Sometimes we see, feel, and experience it. We frequently take it for granted. Occasionally we are so touched by it that our lives are never the same. In other instances, we leave unchanged. As those who follow Jesus, we are called to sharpen our awareness of this community's constant presence, allowing it to continually transform us and our world.

Such discipleship is not easy to sustain. Our media culture encourages us to prefer surface rather than depth. It emphasizes appearance rather than substance, semblance instead of reality. Superficiality triumphs over stability. Madison Avenue markets image, not reality. One company's advertisements proudly announce that "image is everything." We can change our outer appearance and change who we are. If we purchase the right clothes, we become a different person. Our culture encourages us to adopt any surface appearance that appeals to us. Cosmetic surgery has proliferated dramatically in recent years. If we do not like our nose, the curve of our cheek, or the color of our hair, we alter our surface appearance.

Yet religious practice involves depth, not superficiality. Discipleship has to do with authenticity and substance. These are precisely the qualities that our culture of appearance and surface style dismisses as irrelevant. To remain faithful disciples in such a culture requires intentional effort and sustained attention.

How do we cultivate the habits of spirit and qualities of heart that hone our sensitivity to God's ever-present gift of community? How do we nourish our capacity to recognize, celebrate, and invite others to live within God's gracious provision of community?

Distributed Discipleship

We are shaped *for* community *through* community. Context is not just another element in understanding how we grow as Christ's disciples. It is a fundamental factor.

Jerome Bruner observes in *The Culture of Education* that it is a serious mistake to think that our intelligence is lodged inside our own heads.[1] Intelligence exists in the contexts that surround us. We access intelligence through tools we find in these contexts: books, notes, icons, paintings, architecture. Intelligence is located in the heads and habits of people around us. It is distributed in the network of friends, colleagues, companions, and mentors to whom we turn for feedback, help, or advice.

Bruner notes that studies have found that one's chances of winning a Nobel Prize increase dramatically simply by working in a laboratory where someone else has already received a Nobel Prize. It is not because this association gives someone greater visibility or provides "connections." It is not because this association allows for greater intellectual stimulation. Instead, one has entered into an invisible network of relationships whose distributed intelligence now becomes available and accessible.

Human beings are a tool-making and tool-using species. We usually think about "hard tools": chopping stones and digging sticks, hammers and nails, calculators and computers. But we depend just as much upon "soft tools": paintings and books, relationships and conversations. These soft tools allow us to access intelligence, which is, again, not lodged inside our heads but distributed through a communal network of people and objects.

This is why the child can make a mental calculation in the classroom but not in the grocery store. It explains how a student can read a complex game schedule but not understand a classroom reading assignment. It accounts for why the same leader can succeed brilliantly in one setting but fail miserably in another. Knowledge is not primarily in our heads, carried with us from one place to another. Knowledge lies embedded, distributed, in a context. We access it through tools provided by this setting itself.

Perhaps what is true for intelligence is also true for discipleship. We usually think that following Jesus happens inside our own souls, that discipleship involves our individual will and heart, that discipleship is a matter of our personal thoughts, choices, habits, and behaviors. But what if discipleship, like intelligence, is distributed? What if discipleship exists primarily in the context of the community itself? If discipleship is distributed, no one gets into heaven alone. If discipleship is a distributed network in which we participate, there are no solitary Christians.

Through baptism we are joined to a community where God's redemption of all creation is already present and active. We do not baptize ourselves; we are baptized *by* a spiritual community and *for* a spiritual community. Believers do not make themselves members of this community; they are made members. Baptism reminds us that we do not create community by our own efforts. We receive the gift of community and commit ourselves to building up and extending a spiritual community that God has already initiated.

Accessing a Tool Kit for Discipleship

The community itself provides a tool kit of resources and people through which we learn the practices that sustain us as we seek to follow Jesus. When we abide in the vine, we bear fruit. When we lose contact with the vine, our life as disciples withers and dies. "I am the true vine, and my Father is the vinegrower. . . . Abide in me as I abide in you. Just as the branch cannot bear fruit by itself unless it abides in the vine, neither can you unless you abide in me" (John 15:1, 4).

The Gospels hint at how distributed discipleship functioned in Jesus' ministry. When he sent forth the twelve disciples on their missionary journey, Jesus instructed them, "Take no gold, or silver, or copper in your belts, no bag for your journey, or two tunics, or sandals, or a staff; for laborers deserve their food" (Matthew 10:9-10). Jesus' words are extraordinarily limiting. He is sending forth the disciples absolutely defenseless. A staff served not primarily as a support while walking but as a weapon to defend oneself from bandits or wild animals. Swift escape was impossible without sandals. The lack of food and money meant certain starvation along lonely roads.

Jesus' instructions were not possible for individual missionaries traveling alone. But they make perfect sense for itinerant preachers who traveled together and were extended hospitality by a loose network of friends and coworkers. The traveling missionary accessed needed resources by participating in this network of distributed discipleship.

Distributed discipleship means that we are formed *for* community *through* community. The form of our participation in community shapes and reshapes our ability to recognize God's gift of community. The tool kit needed to live in communion with God and others can be accessed through the concrete practices of actual spiritual communities.

Practicing the Faith

John Wesley recognized the fundamental connection between discipleship and community. Many other preachers of the English revival engaged in field preaching. Wesley alone organized his followers into small communities that provided a tool kit of practices and a network of companions. Early Methodists discovered that mutual accountability within a spiritual community effectively built up a consistent discipleship.

Wesley's class meetings focused on practicing the faith. Members held one another mutually accountable for practicing the means of grace. These means of grace were working practices: prayer, reading and meditating on Scripture, observing the Lord's Supper, fasting, Christian conferencing, and concrete acts of compassion and justice.

Wesley felt that assurance of salvation came neither in emotional experiences nor in intellectual assent. Salvation came through adopting concrete practices that led to a new way of life. The priority was not on having a specific religious experience but on pursuing a set of practices that embodied an obedient discipleship.

Similarly, Dietrich Bonhoeffer's meditation on Christian community, *Life Together*, focuses extensively on concrete practices through which we grow in our capacity to experience community in Christ and through which we invite others to share in it.[2] These practices include reading Scripture, praying, singing, celebrating the Lord's Supper, holding one's tongue, meekness, listening, helping, and burden bearing.

These practices of Christian community provide a tool kit of disciplines that sharpen our sensitivity to God's gracious community. They allow us to participate in the distributed discipleship we call the communion of saints and so experience God's gift of communion. These practices shape the desires of our hearts and the longings of our spirit so that we are better able to reach out and invite others into this same blessed communion. Faithful discipleship lies in well-tried practices through which Christians across many generations have opened themselves and others to spiritual community.

Jesus emphasized how concrete practices were essential to membership in God's community. "Everyone then who hears these words of mine and acts on them will be like a wise man who built his house on rock. . . . And everyone who hears these words of mine and does not act on them will be like a foolish man who built his house on sand" (Matthew 7:24, 26). It is a catastrophe to simply listen to Jesus' words. We must also *do* them. Jesus warned that his teachings are something we must do. He was concerned with concrete practice.

What Is a Practice?

The word *practice* has a variety of meanings. To the athlete, practice means repeating an activity to acquire or polish a skill. To the lawyer, practice refers to working at a profession or occupation. To the teacher, practice means drilling students on math facts or the conjugation of verbs. What precisely does the church mean when it speaks of practices?

Practices, according to Alasdair MacIntyre in *After Virtue: A Study in Moral Theory*, have five characteristics:[3]

1. A practice is complex and coherent. Brushing our teeth is not a practice because it is neither complex nor coherent. Fly-fishing, on the other hand, is a practice because it involves a set of complex and coherent actions.
2. People have been doing a practice for a long time. Over time, this activity has evolved through the common effort of many people. One individual may have discovered or identified this practice, but a whole community of people over time has preserved and extended it.
3. We do not undertake a practice merely for the results it produces. A practice is done for its own sake, not merely for its results. Gardening is a practice because people do not garden simply for the results produced. In many cases, we could purchase squash or beans more easily at the local market. People garden for the inherent pleasure of working in the soil, watching plants grow, or enjoying the fresh air.
4. A practice has standards of excellence. Gardening and fly-fishing have generally-agreed-upon standards by which we can determine a good gardener or an expert fly-fisher. If my garden is full of weeds and you cannot see the tomato plants, most gardeners would not classify me as practicing at a very high level. A well-tended garden, on the other hand, is obvious to even a novice practitioner.
5. People continually strive to improve or extend the standards of good practice. A practice is not just an activity that has evolved over time by means of common effort. It is also something that communities of people seek to improve through persistent and consistent effort. The practice of cooking constantly develops as chefs strive to go beyond the present standards to achieve a new level of performance.

Practices of Discipleship

Discipleship involves a number of practices that we acquire, extend, and pursue in the context of Christian community. These practices are created by and are creative of spiritual community in Christ.

Prayer, for example, is something that identifiable groups of people have been doing for centuries. Prayer is something we do for its own sake. We do not pray because we expect particular results to occur, although we rejoice when that happens. Instead, we pray because of the benefits and blessings internal to prayer itself. Prayer, moreover, has some standards by which we recognize excellence. These standards are not the usual standards that the world uses to identify excellence. But we know when a sincere, heartfelt prayer is being offered. Finally, people continually seek to extend the practice of prayer. New ways of praying and new insights into the dynamics of prayer are continually being shared and taught.

Whenever Christians gather, they engage in practices. These practices embody distributed discipleship. They sharpen our awareness of community's presence. They strengthen our capacity to live in ways that embody community.

Some key practices of distributed discipleship for small Christian gatherings include

1. **Listening**. Listening and being listened to are basic ways we acknowledge and recognize one another as sharing a common humanity.
2. **Dialogue.** Through dialogue we create the shared meanings fundamental for community.
3. **Discerning God's will**. Discerning God's will moves us beyond competitive win/lose debate toward a common commitment to God's purposes.
4. **Covenant making**. Covenant making encompasses all the ways we negotiate worthwhile purposes and shared norms together within small groups.
5. **Praying and reflecting together**. Prayer and reflective practice foster a small-group climate where faith formation and spiritual growth are central to whatever the group does.
6. **Hospitality**. Welcoming the stranger keeps Christian small groups from becoming self-serving and inward looking, closed off to God's larger purposes in the world.
7. **Leadership**. Leadership within the Christian community has the cruciform shape of Jesus, who did not cling to authority or lord it over others but instead became a servant.

These practices sharpen our capacity to experience God's gift of Christian community. They increase our ability to reach out and welcome others into spiritual communion with God and others.

Small-Group Practices

We usually pay close attention to the practices of public worship. Careful thought is given to hymns, the order of worship, how communion is served, where banners are hung, or how ushers collect the offering. But as a form of practice that expresses distributed discipleship, public worship does not suffice.

The practices of discipleship also occur in small-group settings that extend far beyond Sunday morning worship. These settings include all the other places and times: accountability groups, support groups, service groups, learning groups, and administrative groups. These settings deserve the same careful attention that we give to our practice of public worship.

Small-group practices actualize the marks of Christian community. They incarnate how Christian community can be Christ-centered, extend hospitality, practice the means of grace, bring wholeness, encourage the discovery of gifts for ministry, and equip people to live out their baptismal covenant.

Small-Group Practices Are the Body of Christ's DNA

The human brain cannot regulate all the body's individual cells. If it tried to monitor and guide each cell, it could do nothing else. Yet the body's millions of cells are managed so that they integrate properly. To accomplish this integration, the body uses a "distributed mind." Just as a computer uses binary code to process information, DNA uses four bases: adenine, guanine, cytosine, and thymine. With just four bases, DNA contains enough information to encode the blueprint for every living thing, from the amoeba to the elephant, from the fruit fly to the human being. Distributed through every cell, DNA acts as a "distributed mind." Each human cell, although specialized, contains information about every other cell. The whole body can therefore be integrated harmoniously.

In the same way, a whole congregation is integrated through distributed discipleship. Using a few basic practices or disciplines, the whole body is unified so that everyone participates in one ministry to every place and people. Combining a few fundamental practices in different ways, each cell of Christ's body has what it needs to carry out its particular ministry. Yet each individual part also manifests the life of the whole.

Each ministry unfolds from the whole congregation's life. And each individual ministry has enfolded within itself a blueprint for the whole congregation. Whenever a small group gathers for service, learning, or administration, the whole congregation is enfolded within it and unfolds from it. Each small-group gathering is enfolded within the whole church and unfolds from it. Discipleship is thus distributed throughout this whole body. A few basic Christian practices or disciplines make this integration possible.

Christian practices are the body of Christ's DNA. These practices have encoded within them enough information for each individual gathering to carry out its specialized ministry. They also carry sufficient information for the fullness of spiritual community to be present when each individual group gathers. Through doing these practices, we give flesh to how we are being a spiritual community that is Christ-centered, extends hospitality, practices the means of grace, brings wholeness, encourages the discovery of gifts for ministry, and equips people to live out their baptismal covenant.

For Further Reflection

Give your congregation's small groups a DNA test. Use the chart on page 34 to list the small groups in your congregation and their communal practices. Then reflect on the following questions:

1. How are the various practices of Christian community present or absent in these groups?
2. What effect does the presence or absence of a practice have on a group?
3. How are the various practices distributed throughout the congregation's small groups? Evenly? Unevenly?
4. What does this exercise suggest as next steps for more effective small-group ministry?

Endnotes

1 See *The Culture of Education*, by Jerome Bruner (Harvard University Press, 1996); page 154.

2 See *Life Together*, by Dietrich Bonhoeffer (Harper & Row, Publishers, Inc., 1954).

3 See *After Virtue: A Study in Moral Theory*, by Alasdair MacIntyre (University of Notre Dame Press, 1984); pages 187–189.

Small Group	Practices	Effect of Practices on Group

Chapter Four

Having Ears to Hear:
The Practice of Listening

Well-tried practices form and transform a people of God. They inscribe particular values and intentions upon our hearts. Each gathering mediates a way of living. Every small group forms the mind of Christ in us and among us. We experience the gift of community and are transformed to live out our baptismal covenant through these practices.

Ironically, marketers and retail anthropologists understand the relationship between values, beliefs, and practices much better than church leaders do. Marketers study how people's values and life structures connect directly to their concrete practices and patterns of consumption. "Tell me your zip code and I'll describe your values and habits," they promise. They scrutinize how attitudes and values—in other words, specific qualities of spirit—are linked to concrete behavioral practices. In order to guide our purchasing practices, their advertisements appeal to what we value or believe about ourselves and the world.

Church organizations sometimes purchase this same demographic marketing information to help them determine where to locate a new congregation or how to revitalize an existing one. Yet they seldom realize the more profound implication: Concrete practices are closely linked to specific values, behaviors, habits, and attitudes. What we do reflects what we value.

Church leaders usually rely upon preaching or teaching to influence how people think and what they value. They give scant attention to the links between specific practices and particular values or beliefs. Perhaps people ignore the church's values, such as tithing, because these disciplines run counter to practices they acquire elsewhere in the culture. Perhaps preaching and teaching are not the only ways to transform lives. Transformation in Christ requires concrete instruction in particular disciplines that shape our habits of spirit and desires of heart.

In the early church, initiation into the Christian community was preceded by a long period of instruction. This instruction did not focus primarily upon doctrine or right belief. It gave priority to how believers practiced the faith. Practice, not belief, verified one's commitment to Christ. To believe is to practice. Doing the truth confirms that we know the truth. "But strive for the greater gifts. And I will show you a still more excellent way," Paul admonishes (1 Corinthians 12:31).

The Practice of Listening

Listening is a basic practice for Christian communities of faith. How we listen reveals how we value ourselves and others. How we listen discloses what we believe about community.

Listening and Community

Listen. With this word, Benedict of Nursia begins his *Rule* for monastic life. For nearly fifteen hundred years, St. Benedict's *Rule* has provided concrete guidance for Christian communal life. It prescribes specific practices and disciplines that sustain Christian community. It is no accident that St. Benedict's *Rule* begins with the word *listen*. Listening is a fundamental practice for Christian communities of faith. All other practices build upon its foundation. Without listening, Christian community is not possible.

Underlying all the other ways that people interact is the fact that speech is our primary mode of relating. Listening and being listened to are basic means of feeling understood and accepted. To listen is to validate, acknowledge, and appreciate another person. People grow through this giving and returning of attention and recognition. Listening and being listened to are the fundamental ways we span the spaces that divide us. The disappointment we feel when we have not been heard reflects how much listening serves as a foundation for our sense of selfhood. Listening is so central to our lives that it often escapes notice. It appears in so many guises that we frequently overlook its importance. Being listened to is how we discover ourselves as acceptable and valuable.

We know God's grace in the experience of listening and being listened to. "Every generous act of giving, with every perfect gift, is from above, coming down from the Father of lights, with whom there is no variation or shadow due to change. . . . You must understand this, my beloved: let everyone be quick to listen, slow to speak, slow to anger" (James 1:17, 19).

We feel sin's presence when we refuse to listen or when we have not been heard.

> Hear this, O foolish and senseless people,
> who have eyes, but do not see,
> who have ears, but do not hear.
> (Jeremiah 5:21)

To listen is to bear witness to community. Through listening we experience communion. Community cannot exist where people are unable or unwilling to listen to each other.

The Challenge of Listening

In spite of listening's critical importance in our lives, few of us are good listeners. A researcher asked a teacher to interrupt her first grade students. She then requested that they write down what they were thinking when she interrupted them. Ninety percent wrote down what the teacher was saying. By second grade, the percentage had dropped to 80 percent. When the same experiment was repeated with a junior high class, only 43.7 percent were listening. Among high school students, a mere 28 percent were listening to the teacher.[1] As we grow older, we forget how to listen.

In fact, some suggest that our educational system actually trains people how not to listen. Teachers instruct students in how to read and write. Young children spend hours learning to add, subtract, multiply, and divide. But no textbook teaches them to listen. Our educational system assumes that the really important skills are writing, reading, and mathematics. Yet most adult leaders will tell you that at least two-thirds of their time is spent listening. Less than one-third is spent writing reports or memos. How do we recover the Christian practice of listening in a society that has forgotten how to listen?

What Is Listening?

To listen well is to bear witness to God's communion among us. Such listening requires disciplined practice.

Listening requires suspending our own agendas, forgetting about what we want to say. Simply holding our tongues while the other person speaks is not the same thing as listening. Listening is attentive receptivity toward another person. To listen we suspend our own agendas and immerse ourselves in the other person. But *suspending* the self does not mean *losing* the self. It means that we go out of ourselves and enter into the world and experience of another person. For a few moments, we exist for and with the other person. Listening involves hospitality. When we listen, we are creating a free, open space where the other person feels welcomed. In this hospitable space, unexpected gifts emerge. When we listen, both we and the speaker are changed forever.

When we listen, we suspend judgment, memory, and desire. Judgment is suspended because we do not give advice. We do not disagree. We do not try to change the other person. Memory is suspended because we do not use the time someone else is speaking to sort through our list of other things to do. We do not think about upcoming events that interest us. Desire is suspended because we control our emotional reactions to statements that make us anxious, uneasy, or uncertain. Anytime we listen with a minimum of defensiveness or criticism or impatience, we give the gift of communion.

Barriers to Listening

Sometimes we find it difficult to listen because people go on and on like they are reciting Tolstoy's *War and Peace*. Others say too little. Some people talk only about their pet topics or preoccupations, beginning to sound like a broken record when we have heard them for the third time. But the trouble with listening usually lies within us, not the other person.

One barrier to listening is *the speech-thought-time differential*. We speak at a rate of 120 to 180 words per minute. But our brains process at the rate of 400 to 800 words per minute. We think three to four times faster than we speak. Our minds are designed to soar, but we talk at a plodding pace. So our minds wander, flit, and race ahead while someone talks. We are easily distracted. We race ahead to the conclusion, guessing how speakers will finish their comments. We pretend to listen but direct our brain to perform other tasks, like composing a letter or compiling a grocery list.

Another barrier to listening is *the emotional filter through which we interpret what we hear*. We hear with our ears, but we listen with our minds. Years ago, our family dog loved to lie beside us and be petted. But occasionally he would growl and snap as we stroked his neck. These episodes were unexpected and seemed unprovoked. We mentioned this behavior to our dog's veterinarian. The vet discovered that our dog had a wound in his neck, possibly from a car accident when he was a puppy. He experienced what we thought was a loving touch as a painful jab. Most of us have similar hidden wounds. When we touch people by speaking to them, they sometimes overreact emotionally; and we sometimes do the same as listeners.

Our preconceptions about the speaker may also filter what we hear. I once held a focused group discussion with some pastors. They unloaded their frustration and anger about the church's "hierarchy" on me because I served as part of the regional church staff. If we listen to someone we perceive to have authority, it can call forth our unresolved issues with all authority figures.

Sometimes we refuse to listen because *we confuse acknowledging someone's feelings with being responsible for how they feel.* We refuse to listen to someone's hurt or pain or anger because we believe that if we listen, we will automatically become responsible for their feelings. Listening to someone talk about their feelings, however, does not make us responsible for those feelings.

Sometimes we choose not to listen because *we confuse listening with agreeing.* We believe that acknowledging a speaker's point of view is the same thing as agreeing with it. But listening and agreeing are two distinct experiences, and we can listen to someone without agreeing with what he or she says. We may need to make this clear at some point in our conversation, depending on the topic and the speaker. But disagreeing does not preclude listening.

Probably the most common barrier to listening is *emotional reactivity.* Emotional reactivity is when we hear something as hurtful, threatening, or infuriating, and we become defensive or even aggressive. It is like throwing a switch and having the electricity come on, but instead of a light bulb's warm glow we get a flashing, blinding strobe light. If you cannot identify what emotional reactivity feels like, remember the last time you ran from the shower to get the telephone, catching it on its last ring. When you picked up the receiver, however, you heard the dial tone. That feeling of agitation is emotional reactivity.

Listening depends on managing our impulse to react emotionally to what someone is saying. But we often respond to others with emotional reactivity, not only in our hearing but also in our speaking. When we express ourselves in highly emotional ways, we can make others anxious and therefore hard of hearing. In this way, emotional reactivity is contagious. It jumps from listener to speaker and escalates and spreads if not contained and cooled.

Emotional reactivity increases as our differentiation from the other person decreases. The closer we are emotionally to another person, the less differentiated we can become. As we become less differentiated, we become more vulnerable to hearing something as hurtful, and thus more prone to emotional reactivity.

Christian congregations involve long-term relationships. Members often experience significant feelings of interpersonal closeness. As a result, boundaries can become blurred. Differentiation decreases, and the probability of emotional reactivity increases.

In emotionally undifferentiated relationships, anxiety becomes infectious. Partners become intensely reactive to one another. When boundaries between people are blurred and individuals are emotionally entangled, almost any emotion will make a listener reactive. Some congregations are like this. Anxiety and reactivity spread quickly. Rather than listening to one another, people engage in emotional cut-offs and angry words. Accusation and counter-accusation are hurled across the room. Blaming and shaming occur. People walk out of the room. They refuse to speak. They pass in the hallway without acknowledging one another.

Learning to listen without overreacting means accepting that each of us is different and separate. We diminish emotional reactivity when boundaries between people are clear and distinct. Paradoxically, we experience communion not when the boundaries between us are collapsed but when we speak and listen as separate, differentiated individuals.

Relationships in genuine Christian community are not directly between people. We have a new focus of relationship in Jesus Christ. We are each related first to Christ, then through Christ we are related to others. We are separate, unique people related through Christ to one another.

When we hold our hands together in prayer, we often press our palms against one another with our fingers stretching heavenward. Our hands point toward Christ. A large part of each hand is in contact with the other, yet our hands remain free to move and flex. Contrast this with how it feels when we intertwine our fingers and clasp our hands. The harder each hand presses against the other, the less either hand can move. The harder each hand clutches at the other, the more painful the experience.

Relationships in community are like two hands held in prayer. Our relationships point beyond themselves to a third party—Jesus Christ. When he is the focus of our relationships, we each remain unique and distinct, yet large parts of our lives can touch and be shared. When boundaries blur, our relationships are more like two hands clutching at one another. A painful tangle locks everything into emotional reactivity.

Perhaps this is what Bonhoeffer means when he suggests that people who love community destroy community. But people who love one another build community.[2] When our goal is emotional fusion, we destroy community. An undifferentiated emotional tangle replaces the richness of community. When we love others in their uniqueness and respect them as individuals separate from us, we create an environment where we can listen to one another. In such environments we experience the gift of community.

Guidelines for Listening

The following are some helpful guidelines for the practice of listening:

1. Remember that listening to others is not the same thing as agreeing with what others are saying. We can listen to others without agreeing with their point of view. We might even learn something. As my grandfather said, "From listening comes wisdom. From speaking comes repentance."

2. Remember that listening to how another person feels is not the same thing as being responsible for how that person feels.

3. Resist the temptation to give advice. When we are giving advice, it usually means that we have let our minds race ahead. We are thinking about a response instead of staying in the present moment and attending to what the speaker is saying.

4. Resist the temptation to tell stories about how we have had the same experience. When we do this, our intentions are usually good. We want to demonstrate to the speaker that we have undergone a similar situation and therefore know how he or she feels. But telling our story shifts the focus away from the speaker. It makes us the center of attention. We are instruments of God's peace when we seek not to be understood but, through listening, to understand another's experiences.

5. Become aware of the hot buttons that prevent us from listening. Hot buttons usually indicate our unresolved wounds. These wounds cause us to filter what speakers are saying. We no longer hear them from their own perspective; we listen through the lens of our own experience. Hot buttons fuel emotional reactivity and make it impossible to listen.

6. Manage our emotional reactivity. People usually give advice such as, "Don't get defensive," for handling emotional reactivity. The problem with such advice is that it is harder to stop doing something than to start doing something else. If we want to stop drinking coffee, it is easier to start drinking tea than to not pour a cup of coffee. Similarly, if we want to reduce our emotional reactivity, it is easier to increase our effort to understand rather than to decrease our defensiveness. If we feel emotionally reactive, we can increase our effort to hear and understand the other person. Rather than focus on the speaker and what a difficult or infuriating person he or she is, we can focus instead on our own efforts to listen. Ask questions. Do not blame. Seek understanding. Anxiety is like electrical current: It requires conduction and amplification. If we listen and stay cool, the other person will feel heard and begin to calm down. When we stay focused on listening, we break emotional reactivity's cycle of contagion.

7. Practice hospitality. Remember that listening is a form of hospitality. By listening, we create a welcoming space where others feel accepted and acknowledged.

Characteristics of Christian Community

The practice of listening fosters the qualities and experiences that characterize Christian community. Listening involves hospitality. When we listen to others, we create a free and open space where they feel welcomed. In such hospitable space, people discover their own true identity. As almost any counselor or therapist will affirm, listening promotes healing and wholeness. When we feel heard, we experience a healing of our spirits.

A good friend tells me that her primary ministry is hearing others into speech. In her presence, people are encouraged to speak. As they do so, they discover gifts and graces for ministry that they never dreamed possible.

The discipline of listening is an ascetic practice. It involves self-denial for the sake of some greater spiritual good or purpose. Listening is hard because it involves a loss of control. When we listen, we become a servant to others. We forget ourselves and our agenda in order to be fully present to the other person.

Let the same mind be in you that was in Christ Jesus,

> who, though he was in the form of God,
> did not regard equality with God
> as something to be exploited,
> but emptied himself,
> taking the form of a slave,
> being born in human likeness.
>
> (Philippians 2:5-7)

Listening requires us to give up being the center of our little world. Listening reminds us that the Christian life has a new focus of relationship in Jesus Christ. With Christ as the third party in every relationship, we can listen openly and graciously to others.

Finally, the church's practice of listening is a discipline we carry over into our daily lives. Whenever and wherever listening happens, grace breaks into our midst. We experience the mystery of spiritual communion. When we practice the discipline of listening in our Christian small-group gatherings, we also learn how to share this gift of listening—and the community it discloses—with those people whose lives we touch in our homes, offices, neighborhoods, and workplaces.

For Further Reflection

Reflect for a few minutes on a time in your life when you felt that someone was truly listening to you.

1. List how you felt in that moment.
2. List what the other person did or said that allowed you to feel heard.
3. Review the small groups in which you participate. How are those qualities and characteristics of listening present? How are they absent?
4. How could you improve the practice of listening in these small groups?

Endnotes

1 See *Perceptive Listening*, by Florence I. Wolff and Nadine C. Marsnik (Harcourt Brace Jovanovich College Publishers, 1992); page 46.

2 See *Life Together*, by Dietrich Bonhoeffer (Harper & Row, Publishers, 1954); pages 28–37.

Chapter Five

Creating Shared Meaning:
The Practice of Dialogue

The practice of dialogue flows naturally from the discipline of listening. Dialogue is a unique spiritual discipline because we can decide on our own to practice it, but we cannot engage in dialogue alone. It requires mutuality, reciprocity, and an open encounter with others.

Because dialogue develops out of our formal and informal conversations, every conversation represents an opportunity for dialogue. Conversations are always happening in congregations: in the parking lot, in the committee meeting, during coffee hour, in the support group, in the choir room. When conversations flower into dialogue, then Christian small groups foster environments where people and their ministries are aligned around common meaning, value, and purpose.

The English word *dialogue* comes from the Greek *dia* and *logos*, meaning "through words." Meaning flows through words in the same way a stream flows between its banks. Dialogue is about the stream of meaning, not the banks of words. Dialogue allows us to bring together our fragmentary, partial perspectives. Through dialogue we discover an underlying wholeness of meaning greater than the sum of our individual viewpoints.

We do not enter into dialogue to solve problems. Through dialogue we create shared meaning. We construct a common understanding that guides collective action.

The Difficulty of Dialogue

Unfortunately, dialogue does not come naturally to modern men and women. We have been reared in a society that some commentators describe as "an argument culture." We assume that the best way to deal with an issue is through the point/counterpoint of debate, that polarization and opposition are the quickest ways to discern the truth. Everything is reduced to a for-or-against position. We glorify our own opinions but demonize our opponents'. We demand respect for our opinions but show no respect for others' opinions.

Our argument culture poses an obvious dilemma. Most issues have more than two sides. Polarization obscures this diversity of opinions. Moderate options are lost when everything is reduced to two opposing extremes.

Christ Church opened its facilities to a Korean fellowship. Church members were soon polarized over whether to continue the relationship. Everyone agreed that problems existed: the building being left unlocked when the Korean fellowship left, use of a loud drum in worship, unfamiliar smells that lingered through the week. But the issue quickly degenerated into two opposing camps. As opinions polarized, those who held more moderate views were shut out of the conversation. In the process, extremism obscured, rather than illuminated, the challenges facing Christ Church. All-or-nothing rhetoric allowed people to overlook the complexity of the issue.

An argument culture creates a self-reinforcing cycle of polarization. Christ Church's increasingly contentious environment attracted people who enjoyed verbal combativeness and political muscle-flexing. Those who did not enjoy verbal combat dropped out.

When a consultant began working with the congregation, both sides had turned their fury on the pastor. "Our attendance is plummeting. No one is coming anymore," they said accusingly. "If we had another pastor, our inactive members would come back." These inactive members, when interviewed by the consultant, said that they liked the pastor and were supportive of her ministry. But they were tired of the bickering and squabbling. They no longer wished to invest energy in a conflicted congregation.

The church of Jesus Christ too often mirrors our argument culture. It seldom represents a transforming presence that bears witness to another vision of human community. Confrontation and polarization do not produce community. In the short run, they may generate a pseudo-community united in common opposition to someone or something. Polarization and divisiveness, however, run counter to God's vision of a new communion of love encompassing all creation.

Our argument culture reflects a deeper crisis in how we view the world. We have learned to divide and fragment our world. We chop reality into bits and pieces, which we then categorize into tidy pigeonholes. Because we focus on unrelated parts and do not see the whole, our thinking is fragmentary. This fragmentary thinking gives rise to a picture of the world that constantly breaks up into disharmonious, partial activities set in opposition to each other.

Supporters of the Korean ministry at Christ Church saw only the people being reached with the good news of Jesus Christ. Opponents saw only the messy kitchen or the unlocked windows. Everyone saw parts. No one saw the whole. When our thinking is partial and fragmentary, we see all the positive aspects of our position and all the negative aspects of our opponent's proposal. We fail to acknowledge that our viewpoint has some negative consequences. We refuse to recognize the positive consequences to our opponent's proposal.

We lose sight of how everything is connected and whole. We set one fragment in opposition to another. We forget the God-given unity that underlies all things. "Hear, O Israel: the Lord our God, the Lord is one; you shall love the Lord your God with all your heart, and with all your soul, and with all your mind, and with all your strength. . . . You shall love your neighbor as yourself" (Mark 12:29-31). Great wisdom sees all in one. Small knowledge breaks things down into many parts. When we divide reality into bits and pieces, we lose sight of the subtle ties that bind together the web of life. We are not separate; we are instead mysteriously interconnected at some deep level that is itself the gift of God's communion.

Perceiving a Deeper Unity

When electrons are cooled to a very low temperature, they cease acting like separate entities and behave like a coherent whole. The higher the temperature, the more they act like separate parts. They move in random, scattering patterns. Similarly, the hotter our conflicts, the more we fragment and divide. When we enter into the "cooling container" of God's presence, we experience the unity and oneness of communion. Our thoughts become aligned, less scattered, less fragmented. We stop seeing the parts and perceive the whole.

We usually approach our differences by seeking a compromise between opposing positions. We engage in tradeoffs and dealmaking. At Christ Church, one side was willing to let the Korean fellowship stay if the fellowship doubled its monthly payment to the church and agreed to stop playing drums in the building. The other side was willing to hire a custodian to clean the building on Sunday night after the Koreans left. Each group tried to bargain, negotiate, or compromise around turf they had already staked out for themselves.

Dialogue operates from a different premise. In dialogue we are not trying to negotiate or bargain. We seek to discover the underlying wholeness. This wholeness already exists. Our partial, fragmentary vision has simply obscured its presence.

Dialogue requires not just participative openness but reflective openness. Participative openness means that we let everyone speak his or her mind, but we may or may not listen because our minds are already made up. Everyone feels that he or she has a right to his or her own opinion, yet no one listens to anyone else.

Reflective openness, on the other hand, involves a willingness to challenge our own thinking. We remain open to examining our own assumptions, no matter how uncomfortable doing so may feel. Dialogue is not interested in focusing down until the group finds the least common denominator. It seeks instead to open up and out toward a meaning larger than any single participant's viewpoint.

Dialogue encourages people to enter into a pool of shared meaning that leads to aligned action. We participate in a flowing stream of common meaning. This stream is capable of constant development and change as our dialogue unfolds. It has both its source and its goal in God.

In one scene of the movie *Dances With Wolves*, the Lakota leaders sit around a campfire. They are talking, but the conversation does not seem to go anywhere. No decisions are made. Long periods of silence are punctuated by a few words. Nothing seems accomplished. A few minutes later the movie shows these same leaders on a buffalo hunt. The riders move in effortless synchronization with one another. One hunter seems to anticipate the moves of another. I suddenly realized as I watched these scenes that this perfect alignment of independent actions was possible only because of the dialogue around the campfire. Everyone was participating in a shared, common mind that emerged through the process of dialogue. This shared meaning was the invisible leader that guided and aligned the hunters' individual actions.

When I read the story of the Jerusalem Council in Acts 15, I see it through the lens of *Dances With Wolves*. Paul, Barnabas, Peter, James, John, and others are gathered together in Jerusalem. They come with their fragmentary visions of what God is doing. Some think Gentile converts should be circumcised; others think circumcision denies Christ's grace. They tell their stories. They listen. They enter into the flow of dialogue. They dip down into a deeper pool of shared meaning that bubbles with God's creativity and grace. The council arrives at a solution that seems right to them and to the Holy Spirit. Each apostle then goes from the circle to his or her individual ministry. These ministries are aligned with one another, even though they are widely scattered, because they are all of one mind and one spirit.

The Process of Dialogue

Conversations are always happening in congregations. Formal and informal conversations occur whenever and wherever small groups gather. Each gathering thus becomes an opportunity for dialogue. The practice of dialogue follows a predictable sequence in all these settings.

As people discuss their opinions about a situation or a topic, they quickly realize how divergent their opinions are. Some members of a Sunday school class take Genesis' creation story literally; others see it as symbolic. Some members of a service group feel that "you will always have the poor with you" (Matthew 26:11); others believe that God's creation offers an abundance of good things for all people, but we in our sinfulness create a culture of scarcity.

Participants are usually unaware of these fragmentary perspectives and partial viewpoints. They are tacit and assumed. As people talk, these differences become visible and the conversation can go in two directions. (See figure below.)

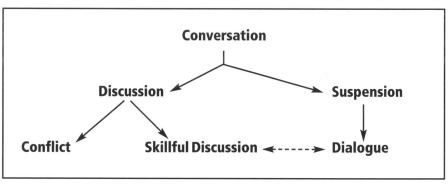

People may choose sides and begin to defend their own viewpoint, dismissing all other perspectives. When this happens, the group falls into a discussion rather than a dialogue. *Discussion* comes from the same Latin root as words like *percussion* or *concussion*. It means, literally, to shake apart. When we discuss something, we bat ideas back and forth. We avoid facts that contradict our viewpoints. We refuse to challenge our own opinions. Discussion, if not well-managed, can become emotionally reactive. It can degenerate into a full-blown conflict.

We know that we have lapsed into conflict when people begin labeling their opponents. At Christ Church, supporters of the Korean fellowship automatically labeled the opposition as racist. Labeling people denies the legitimacy of their opinions. It makes further discussion unnecessary. Name calling means our minds are made up. We no longer see our opponents as worthy of respect. When we engage in name calling, we break one of the Ten Commandments. We bear false witness against another person.

Groups have opted for conflict over dialogue when they attribute unworthy motives to their opponents. They think they know their opponents' true motives regardless of what they say or do. Supporters of the Korean fellowship had requested a consultant to help resolve the conflict. The members who made this request saw themselves as seeking a positive outcome to what had become an ugly conflict. Their opponents claimed the real motive was to postpone a vote on whether the Korean fellowship could remain in the building. Nothing alienates and angers people more than to have their motives questioned or their integrity maligned. What would happen if we began with the assumption that our opponents' motives were as sincere and well-intentioned as our own?

Our conversations need not always lapse into discussion or conflict. Participants may decide to loosen the grip of their certainty and suspend their perspectives, letting their assumptive worlds hang out in the open. From this vantage point, everyone can examine these fragmented mental models of how the world is put together. But suspending assumptions is a scary experience. It feels like chaos. Everything becomes unstable.

At this point, group members may feel frustrated or even frightened. The underlying incoherence of everyone's thought—including their own—becomes apparent. No single point of view seems to hold all the truth. No conclusions seem valid. The group has entered what some facilitators call "the groan zone." All the fragmentation that is usually hidden becomes apparent.

At Christ Church, the consultant structured a session where the two opposing groups talked about their differences. Everyone began to feel uncomfortable as the conversation unfolded. As perspectives were suspended where everyone could examine them, people slowly realized how fragmentary and partial their positions really were.

Supporters of the Korean fellowship wondered if the congregation was healthy enough to enter into a relationship with another culture. Opponents of the ministry expressed how they were envious that the Korean fellowship was growing while their own congregation was shrinking. This group of strangers might end up owning a building that their parents and grandparents had sacrificed to build. The unlocked windows and the messy kitchen were not the real issues. Their own fear and resentment made it difficult to accept the Korean congregation in the building.

If a critical mass of participants stays engaged, the group may move into dialogue. People move beyond labels. They begin thinking about how they think. Dialogue's objectives are exploration, discovery, and insight. Along the way, the group may reach some agreement. But that is not dialogue's primary purpose. Dialogue seeks to create shared meaning from which everyone may draw new purpose and meaning.

Midway between dialogue and conflict lies another alternative: skillful discussion. Skillful discussion uses many of the same tools as dialogue. The goal, however, is not to create new meaning. It is to make a decision, develop a plan, solve a problem, or reach a conclusion. Skillful discussion provides a "cool container" that lowers emotional reactivity. Everyone can make his or her thought processes visible, bring assumptions to the surface, and understand the sources that underlie disagreement. It becomes easier to solve problems or reach decisions in such an environment.

Tools for Dialogue and Skillful Discussion

A primary tool for both dialogue and skillful discussion is one's own self-awareness:

• What am I thinking?
• What am I feeling?
• What do I want right now?

A second tool for dialogue and skillful discussion is paying attention to one's own intentions:

• What are my intentions in this conversation? What do I want to happen?
• Am I willing to be influenced? If not, what is the purpose of the conversation?

One sign of emotional reactivity is an inability to separate our feelings from our thoughts. When we are emotionally reactive, our feelings short-circuit our thinking. We start blaming others and leave the self out of the picture. We are unable to see how our actions contribute to the situation. When we refocus separately on thinking and feeling, we begin to distance ourselves emotionally from the situation. We free ourselves from being stuck in reactivity when we ask about the self and its role and responsibility.

We lift ourselves from emotional reactivity by raising everyone's thinking capacity. The skillful use of questions raises thinking capacity. Good questions help us see the world in a new way. One of God's first recorded remarks to humankind is a question: "Adam, where are you?" (Genesis 3:9). Jesus repeatedly used questions to open his hearers to new perspectives and see themselves and their world in new ways: Whose picture is on this coin? Who is the neighbor? What are you seeking? What do you want? Who do people say that I am?

Perhaps the apostles' many conversations with Jesus account for how they could individually scatter across the Roman world and yet remain one in mission. As they walked along the roads of Galilee or sat together for table fellowship, Jesus transformed these conversations into dialogues in which the disciples were caught up in a larger stream of meaning, vision, and purpose. They drank from one common stream of God's meaning and purpose. So when they carried the gospel from Jerusalem to Judea and Samaria and all the ends of the earth, their individual ministries remained aligned with one common purpose and vision.

Dialogue and Christian Community

Whenever small groups gather, conversations happen. The support group, the learning group, the service group, and the administrative group all rely upon the give-and-take of conversation. These small-group settings represent opportunities for dialogue, discussion, or conflict.

The midweek Bible study can divide over the authority and interpretation of Scripture. The administrative council can be wracked by conflict over whether the church should alter the character of Sunday morning worship. Some settings lend themselves more obviously to dialogue than to conflict. The accountability group, for example, is more likely to experience dialogue than discussion. Members usually come to the support group expecting dialogue, not conflict. Yet all these settings are potential opportunities to experience the miracle of dialogue.

Once leaders become conscious of the potential for dialogue, they can promote practices that encourage dialogue rather than discussion, skillful discussion rather than conflict. When small-group members engage in dialogue, they experience the gift of Christian community.

We all know how inhospitable a group wracked by conflict feels. Conversely, a group that practices dialogue extends hospitality to participants. Conflict rends asunder. It divides and breaks apart. Dialogue, on the other hand, promotes wholeness. Dialogue heals the divisions between us.

When we allow conflict to characterize our spiritual communities, we put ourselves and our opinions at the center. We have placed how strongly we are committed to our opinions, rather than how deeply we are committed to Christ, at the center of our thinking. The practice of dialogue reminds us that we and our opinions are not at the center of community. Christ is.

Like the tribal elders in *Dances With Wolves* or the apostles at the Jerusalem Council, we are equipped and aligned for ministry when dialogue characterizes our gatherings. Having constructed a shared meaning, we are empowered to live out our baptismal covenant with renewed enthusiasm.

For Further Reflection

The chart on page 54 gives examples of questions that promote inquiry and advocacy. How could you use these guidelines and questions to improve how you inquire into your own assumptions as well as those of others? How could you use them to better advocate for your point of view or encourage others to advocate for theirs?

Use the chart to help you monitor your conversations this week. Make a serious attempt to move toward dialogue with at least one person or group. What was this experience like for you? Did you notice any changes in yourself? Did you notice any changes in the other person?

How could you encourage the practice of dialogue in more settings and groups within your congregation?

Inquiry

Principle	Example
Find out the data on which others are operating.	What leads you to that conclusion? What are your reasons for saying that?
Help others explore their reasoning without sounding like you are interrogating.	What is the significance of that? How is that important? How does that matter? What are you assuming when you . . . ?
Seek to understand the experiences out of which they arrived at their views.	Tell me the experiences that shaped how you look at this.
Explain your reasons for inquiry.	I want to better understand and learn from your conclusions, so could you help me . . . ?
Ask the person to compare his or her point of view with another.	How is this response different from *Name*'s response? Who might see this differently from you? Why would they have different assumptions?

Advocacy

Principle	Example
State your assumptions and your data.	I assumed that . . . I came to this conclusion because . . .
Encourage others to explore your data.	What are some of the consequences of what I have said? How have we used the same data differently?
Reveal where you are least clear in your thinking.	Here is something you might help me think through.

Chapter Six

To Will One Will:
The Practice of Discerning God's Will Together

O ur family loves to fly kites in the meadow behind our home. The kites bob, dip, and soar above our heads. The ancient Chinese, who invented and flew the first kites, did not treat kites as child's play. They used them to signal troop movements during battle. The Chinese also regarded kites as tools for prayer and meditation: As we practice responding to the wind's shifting currents, we learn to live in harmony with life's ever-changing rhythms.

Preachers proclaim that the winds of God's Spirit are always blowing. We need only to hoist our sails and catch the breeze. Yet catching this spiritual wind is not as easy as it sounds. The wind beneath my physical kite constantly shifts, moves, and changes. It suddenly changes direction, and my kite spirals precipitously downward. I frantically pull the string, hoping to catch another current to carry it upward. The wind above our meadow is a living thing. The west wind turns and blows from the south. It gains speed and loses momentum. My family's kites remain aloft because we are continually responding to these ever-changing winds. The same is true for catching the winds of God's Spirit.

To discern God's will is to move in rhythm with the deep, ever-changing winds of God's Spirit. This is the goal and purpose of Christian existence. We discern God's will so that we can make wise choices that move in harmony with God's life-giving energies. "What is born of the flesh is flesh, and what is born of the Spirit is spirit. . . . 'You must be born from above.' The wind blows where it chooses, and you hear the sound of it, but you do not know where it comes from or where it goes. So it is with everyone who is born of the Spirit" (John 3:6-8). Discernment concerns the discovery of God's specific word to us in the ever-changing circumstances of our lives.

Discernment Is Not Divination

Discernment is not the same as divination. Ancient peoples examined a sheep's entrails or watched the flight of birds to discover what their gods had preordained. The will of the gods was already decided. Humans were pawns who accomplished predetermined divine purposes.

Divination seeks to uncover decisions about our lives that God has already made. It presupposes a spatial and temporal distance between ourselves and God. God is "up there." We are "down here." God has previously ordained what will happen. We are divining what has already been predetermined.

But we cannot find God's will in a sheep's liver or a bird's flight. God's will is written on our hearts, not in the constellations. We discover God's will in the concrete flow of our daily experiences, not in the movement of planets. God's will "is not in heaven, that you should say, 'Who will go up to heaven for us, and get it for us so that we may hear it and observe it?' . . . No, the word is very near to you; it is in your mouth and in your heart for you to observe" (Deuteronomy 30:12, 14).

We can discern the shape of God's will for our lives because all the different dimensions of our lives interact and are interdependent. When we move toward or away from God at the deepest levels of our being, this movement has repercussions in our surface awareness. Conscious thoughts and emotions thus reveal what is happening at interior levels not immediately available to our awareness. Discernment involves monitoring these moods, thoughts, emotions, and affections for what they reveal about deeper movements either toward or away from God and God's intentions.

The Limits of Discernment

There are at least two limits on discerning God's will. First, we can only discern what God intends for *us* to do. We cannot discern what God intends for someone else to do. Trying to know God's plans for someone else is divination, not discernment. It presumes divination's temporal and spatial distance from human life: God has already preordained the facts of someone's life. We can therefore gaze into a crystal ball and divine what will happen to that person.

This limitation is a necessary precondition for group discernment. When we believe that God has told us what others should do, we cannot listen openly to their viewpoints. And nothing ends dialogue faster than telling people that you know what they ought to do. The practice of discernment allows no room for self-righteousness and arrogance.

Second, we cannot discern what may happen in the future. Discernment involves only what God intends for us to choose in this specific situation at this particular moment. Jane discerns that God intends for her to become a missionary. She volunteers for missionary service. As part of her application, Jane has a physical exam. The doctor discovers that she has a heart condition that prevents her from qualifying as a missionary. Jane now doubts her initial discernment. She becomes disillusioned, feeling that God has misled her.

We cannot know what God intends for the future. We can only discern what God wills for us to choose here and now. To seek to know the future is divination, not discernment. Perhaps God intended for Jane to choose to become a missionary precisely so that she would go to a doctor. Perhaps God intended for Jane to choose to become a missionary so that her example would inspire someone else to volunteer for missionary service. Jane cannot know God's ultimate intentions; she can only discern what God intends for her to choose in this particular circumstance.

Settings and Guidelines for Discernment

Discernment occurs in at least three settings. One of these settings is personal and individual. The other two are group activities. In the first setting, we individually discern God's will for our personal lives. In the second setting, a group helps us clarify or confirm a personal discernment. A support group, for example, may help one of its members discern God's will for his or her life. In the third setting, a formal group seeks God's will together for its common life. Members of a service group, for instance, may discern what God intends for the group to choose as their next project.

All three settings for discernment depend upon the following basic spiritual concepts. Discernment arises from an awareness of these principles.

Desires and Attachments

Discernment demands a thorough knowledge of self. We cannot know God's will when we do not even know ourselves. The soul cannot know a nature beyond itself without first knowing its own desires and impulses.

Unconscious, hidden desires give birth to attachments. An attachment is a desire in which we are highly invested. These attachments hold us back and paralyze us. Disordered attachments are a fundamental barrier to discerning God's will. They add a quality of drivenness to our desires.

If we are attached to our desire to appear successful, we fear failure. We consequently refuse tasks that involve the risk of failure. Yet these tasks may be the very ones to which God calls us. If we are attached to our desire for acceptance, we fear rejection. We are therefore reluctant to share ourselves in relationships. Consequently we cut ourselves off from the very people with whom God wishes us to be in communion.

Hidden desires and attachments also distort our perceptions of reality. Without reliable perceptions of reality, we cannot discern where God is working in our lives. We are so attached to what we want that we turn away from what God intends. We confuse our own interior voices for God's voice. The less we know ourselves, the more seductive these competing voices become.

Small hidden attachments are more dangerous than great temptations. We are at least aware of the great temptations with which we struggle. A small attachment, on the other hand, possesses enormous power to distort our perceptions and compel our behavior. In *Ascent of Mount Carmel*, St. John of the Cross compares hidden attachments to a remora, or suckerfish. During the sixteenth century, wind-powered ships could be rendered motionless at sea by a lack of wind. Sailors blamed the suckerfish for this problem. They believed that small suckerfish attached themselves to ships and held them stationary. So it is with people, John observed. They are like ships loaded with rich treasures of good works, virtues, and prayer. Yet one small, hidden attachment can keep them from advancing in the spiritual life.

A small speck of dust can clog a clock's gears and throw off its ability to keep time. In the same way, small attachments can throw off our perceptions. When our perceptions are warped or distorted, we cannot accurately discern how God is moving in our lives.

A man arrives at the airport only to discover that his flight is showing a movie he has already seen. He hears that another airplane is showing the very movie he wants to see, so he changes his ticket and takes the second flight. When the plane lands, he finds himself in a strange city without friends or purpose. An impulsive attachment distorted his perceptions and controlled his choices.

Knowing our hidden desires also has a positive consequence. Our desires are the best clues we have to our true self. We are what we desire. We become what we love. And that is how we grow. Our great desires lift us beyond our own selfish needs and wants. These great desires are usually at one with God's desires. As we come to know these deepest desires, we better discern God's desires for us and for our world.

When we are exploring our desires, we are not examining our motives. The focus is not on past or present motives behind our actions. We observe the immediate feelings and affective impulses that we are experiencing here and now. These affections are usually described as consolations or desolations.

Consolations and Desolations

It would be easy to discern God's will if we simply equated pleasant feelings with consolations and unpleasant feelings with desolations. Unfortunately, discernment is not so simple. The meaning of a particular feeling depends upon the general direction of our relationship with God. So the same impulse or feeling can mean opposite things. (See chart below.)

Orientation Toward God

	Turned Away	Turned Toward
Consolations	Painful dislocation, sorrow, regret, guilt, failure, contrition	Peace, harmony, grace, joy
Desolations	Self-confidence, complacency, self-satisfaction, pleasure	Confusion, anger, apathy, sense of abandonment by God, discouragement

When we are out of tune with God, we experience negative feelings as consolations. Negative experiences are consolations because they awaken our yearning for God. Good spirits cause us to be unhappy about our lives when we are out of tune with God. They challenge us to examine our lives. They jar us out of smug self-confidence and invite us to change the direction of our lives.

In the same way, pleasant feelings are desolations when our lives are turned away from God. Pleasant feelings distract us from our relationship with God. They amuse us so that we do not reflect on the deeper consequences of our behavior.

When our lives are oriented toward God, on the other hand, consolations and desolations have their more typical meaning. Pleasant feelings are consolations. They comfort and reassure us of God's grace and love. Negative experiences such as malaise or apathy are desolations. They cause us to question our trust in God's care and presence.

A deep sense of inner peace is the primary mark of consolation. Evil spirits usually come crashing, roaring, and shouting. They spread confusion, anger, and hostility. Good spirits bring tranquility and quiet assurance. Yet inner peace is a tricky guide. We can mislabel a superficial sense of relief at resolving a troubled situation as consolation's deep peace. We can feel tremendous relief on the surface of our lives even when our inner spirit is still troubled. On the other hand, we can feel a deep peace about a decision even when it creates turmoil in our immediate experience. We experience spiritual consolations at this deep level, not in superficial relief.

Juan felt a sense of relief when he finally reached a decision about taking a new job. He had struggled for several days about what to do. He felt pulled, first this way and then another. This sense of relief felt like inner peace about his choice. A few months later, Juan felt betrayed by his discernment. The job was not turning out as he had expected. Juan had confused an immediate sense of relief at reaching a decision with consolation's sense of inner peace.

We also need to distinguish consolation's inner peace from the afterglow that follows it. Peter had a moment of consolation when he recognized Jesus as the Messiah at Caesarea Philippi. Just a few verses later, Jesus told the disciples he would go to his death in Jerusalem. Peter then refused to accept Jesus' prediction of his death. Peter's initial discernment, in which he recognized Jesus as the Messiah, occurred in a moment of consolation. His second discernment, in which he argued with Jesus, happened in its afterglow.

Carla went on a work trip to Haiti. During a particular prayer service, she experienced a profound sense of peace and purpose. When she returned home, she felt called to quit her job and work with the poor. She took a position at a homeless shelter for a much lower salary. Gradually, Carla found herself more and more depressed and frustrated. Eventually she resigned and returned to her former work. The whole experience left her bitter and angry. Carla's consolation was real, but her decision to quit her job and work at the homeless shelter was made not under her consolation's influence but during its afterglow. When individuals and groups make choices during a consolation's afterglow, they can confuse their will for God's will.

We can sometimes experience false consolations. Martina had a powerful spiritual experience on a retreat. Afterward, she felt drawn to a deeper prayer life. She added an extra hour of prayer to her daily schedule, getting up earlier each morning. She eventually began to suffer sleep deprivation. Physically weakened, her whole life suffered. She was often either too tired or too sick to pray. Gradually she stopped attending her Covenant Discipleship Group, saying she was not feeling well. She began to sleep late on Sundays rather than attend worship. Eventually Martina dropped out of her congregation and its small groups.

Individuals and groups need to examine carefully experiences that appear to be consolations. They may be false consolations that can wreak havoc in our lives.

A desolation is the opposite of a consolation. When we are oriented toward God, desolations cause us to feel weighed down or in turmoil. Our spirit is restless and cannot find peace. Anger and fear dominate. These powerful negative emotions can destroy the inner harmony necessary for discernment.

If it is possible, individuals and groups should make no major decisions when gripped by desolations. This is simple but profound advice. Many of us have seen people or groups make terrible decisions during times of grief, depression, frustration, anger, or conflict.

Refraining from making decisions during times of desolation, however, does not mean that we should do nothing. Whenever we are suffering through such periods of desolation, we can remember times of consolation.

Individuals and groups can also follow the advice of Evagrius Ponticus, a monastic theologian of the fourth century, and do the exact opposite of whatever action our affective impulses urge upon us. When we are tempted to seek solitude, we can spend more time with our companions. When we are tempted to skip our prayers, we can pray twice as long.

Another appropriate action is to find a spiritual companion to walk through the experience with us. Desolations, like most negative experiences, can be very lonely. In such moments we need someone who can give us a perspective on our struggles. Desolations and secrets go hand in hand. We are truly as sick as our secrets. An evil spirit encourages secrecy. The best tactic is to share with spiritual companions any thoughts that come to us during times of desolation, bringing secrets into the light of day.

Finally, we can practice the spiritual disciplines of prayer and Scripture reading. Persistence in prayer carries us through times when we feel desolate and dislocated. While we should not make decisions that change our life situations during times of desolation, we can focus on changing ourselves through prayer, meditation, the study of Scripture, and good works.

Using Imagination or Reason

When we are not tossed about by strong consolations or desolations, individuals and groups may best discern God's will by using their imagination and creativity. We can imagine ourselves in a conversation with a stranger who describes the situation we are facing. We then listen to our reply. Or we can imagine ourselves standing before Christ and giving an account of our lives. As our life story unfolds, we come to this specific situation that we are seeking discernment for. What do we hear ourselves telling Christ?

When we lack experiences of consolation or desolation, individuals and groups can use their reason to discern God's will. We can draw up a list of advantages and disadvantages and ask which contribute most to God's glory and praise. In other words, we explore which option is most faithful, not which is most reasonable or efficient or effective. Does this option increase our freedom as God's children? Does it promote growth in Christ? Does it draw us closer to others and to God? Is it consistent with Scripture and tradition?

Making a Choice

When we think about discernment, we usually focus only on the act of choosing. But getting ready to choose—not the choice itself—is the difficult, time-consuming work. Discernment lies as much in preparing to choose as in the choice itself. Preparations include understanding the self, with its attachments and desires; paying attention to affective impulses such as consolations and desolations; and using our reason and imagination. Once we have made these preparations, the decision itself is usually the easy part.

As individuals and groups meditate on their gathered evidence of affective impulses, attachments, and imagination or reason, they never reach a conclusion based on a single testimony or experience. When I lived on Cape Cod, I occasionally took the ferry to Nantucket. Returning at night, I could see the lighthouses twinkling on a distant shore. I could hear the buoys ringing as they rocked in the waves. Standing on deck, I realized that the captain did not find the harbor by using any single lighthouse. The captain instead located the ferry's position by reference to several lighthouses.

In the same way, discerning God's will requires that we locate ourselves in relation to several signposts, not just one. If we have sought guidance by reflecting on consolations and desolations, then we submit our tentative conclusions to reason and imagination. If we have relied upon logic and reason, then we plumb the depths of our hearts for interior movements.

We look for signs of spiritual consolation. We seek an intensification of our will that expresses itself in an eagerness to implement our choice. We inquire into new reasons that confirm a choice. We search for greater force in the existing reasons we have compiled.

Above all else, individuals and groups wait for a deep assurance that they have done everything possible to seek God's will. This assurance is ultimately not about the correctness of the final decision. It refers instead to a conviction that we have done everything possible to reach a conclusion pleasing to God. Until we have this assurance, we wait for more evidence to accumulate, for stronger affective impulses to move our wills, or for a deeper clarification of what God intends for us to choose. We continue our discernment.

In the end, our confidence resides neither in our consolations nor in our reasoning. It rests in our faith that God gives us the Spirit to guide and empower our lives. This basis for certainty is both liberating and leveling. It is liberating because we do not bear the burden of depending on our own resources. Our confidence is in God's gracious provision, not in ourselves. This basis for certainty is leveling because no single person has any greater access to the Spirit than another. The simplest Christian can know God's will as well as the greatest mystic.

Group Discernment to Help Individuals

As we seek to know God's will, we sometimes invite a group of Christian friends to help us clarify God's intentions in a particular situation. Their comments can correct, revise, expand, or confirm our own discernment. We are not asking the group to solve our problems for us. We are not requesting advice. We are asking the group to create a climate where we can better hear God's personal word to us.

This process is profoundly countercultural. It assumes that the greatest help we give others is to refrain from fixing their problems for them. When people struggle to find God's will for their lives, their anxieties and fears sometimes overpower them. Anxious people often try to rid themselves of these anxieties and bind them to others. They shift their emotional burdens onto others. When we give advice or try to fix other people's problems, we are taking responsibility for them rather than being responsive to them.

Jesus had compassion for people, but he refused to let them shift their anxiety-laden emotional burdens onto him. Martha was anxious about dinner preparations. She rushed here and there. She fussed and fretted. She tried to shift the burden of her anxieties and fears onto Jesus: "Look at all I am doing! Make Mary help me." Jesus was responsive to Martha. He acknowledged her anxiety. He had compassion for her. But he refused to take responsibility for her feelings. He did not jump up and start peeling carrots or making gravy. He refused to order Mary into the kitchen. He instead gave information and stirred Martha's imagination (Luke 10:38-42).

Jesus models how spiritual companions help others discern God's will. The group serves as a nonanxious presence. Group members are clear about boundaries, responsibilities, and goals. They self-differentiate. They respond without taking responsibility. The group does not overfunction. It does not rescue. It raises the individual's capacity for discernment by posing questions, offering another angle of vision, and raising the inquirer's thinking capacity.

Group guidance is not a formless process in which some Christian friends get together on the spur of the moment to discuss a problem. It has a particular structure and format. (See box on page 64.)

Process for Group Discernment to Help an Individual

- Choose participants.
- Prepare background statement.
- Participants review statement and engage in personal discernment.
- Convene meeting with silence and prayer.
- Establish group norms.
- Review and update background statement.
- Pose questions.
- Open dialogue.
- Close with prayer.
- Continue discernment and prayer.

Setting the Context

The person asking for assistance bears the burden of setting the context for group guidance. When we invite a group to help us discern God's will, we have a special responsibility to provide participants with the information they need. We also remain open to what they say. We do not become argumentative or defensive.

Group members have their own part to play. They take time to pray about the situation before they gather. They respect the presenter's experience. They are present to listen, not to give advice. They do not impose solutions or make authoritative statements. When asking probing questions, members refrain from being inquisitive for curiosity's sake.

Preparing a Statement of the Concern

Preparing a statement of the concern is the first step in a communal discernment. Group members require background information. This information helps them individually discern what God intends for them to say.

The person presenting the concern is responsible for assembling a statement that participants can use as they pray and discern individually. This statement provides participants with necessary background information. What led up to this situation? What dynamics impinge upon it? Who are the relevant parties? It outlines the major issues and options as the presenter perceives them. The presenter distributes this statement to all participants before the group session. Participants need time to reflect on the statement and to engage in their own personal discernment.

Meeting Together

After group members have had time to engage in personal discernment, the group gathers. This meeting begins with a period of silence. Silence invites people to let go of their own preconceptions, to place the outcome of the discussion in God's hands, and to ask for sensitive hearts and minds. A brief spoken prayer gathers these themes and ends the silent preparation.

Someone designated as the group's facilitator next reviews a list of norms for the session. One absolutely essential norm is confidentiality. Without confidentiality, trust cannot exist, and communication will be sanitized and guarded. Other norms might include refraining from criticism, refraining from giving advice, and refraining from being judgmental.

Once the group has affirmed its norms, the person presenting the concern makes an introductory statement. This statement reviews the information previously given to the group. It also includes new experiences, insights, or thoughts that may have arisen since the written statement was distributed.

When the presenter finishes the introductory statement, others begin to raise issues or to pose questions. The goal is to listen the other person into speech, disclosure, and discovery. During this portion of the session, participants can only ask questions; they cannot make statements. This questions-only rule prevents people from giving advice or "preaching at" the presenter.

The presenter is free to respond to these questions or to remain silent. The session is not an interrogation in which the presenter responds to every question. The purpose is to listen for God's Spirit speaking in the group's midst.

This time of asking questions and responding may continue until participants feel that no more important issues are surfacing. At this point, the questions-only rule may be relaxed. Participants are free to talk about what they have heard or felt during the meeting. They may share insights that came to them about their own lives. They may recite a poem or portion of Scripture that came to mind during the session. Again, group members share from their own experience; they do not advise or admonish.

A closing prayer ends the session. Afterward the presenter proceeds with his or her own discernment. Group members continue to keep the presenter in their prayers.

Practicing Communal Discernment

The goal of communal discernment is not to arrive at a decision that has the most persuasive backing or that a majority will find acceptable. Communal discernment incorporates many elements of consensus building, yet discernment cannot be identified or confused with making decisions by consensus.

Communal discernment's goal is to seek God first and then to discover God's will. In finding God, we also find God's will. The primary goal of communal discernment is to enable the group to be aware of and respond to the presence of God's Spirit in their midst.

God operates through a calculated inefficiency. No one has all the truth. Everyone has a part of the truth. We only discover the whole of God's truth when we enter into prayerful, open listening and dialogue with God and one another.

Preconditions for Communal Discernment

Communal discernment cannot occur until at least seven preconditions exist. These preconditions allow for the Spirit's freedom. They are the seedbed in which discernment flourishes.

First, *communal discernment is possible only where members of the community already practice discernment in their individual lives.* All the elements of individual discernment find a place in communal discernment: serious and prolonged prayer, a thorough knowledge of the situation, a freedom regarding the outcome, a search for reasons for and against the option, a sensitivity to consolations and desolations. Communal discernment presupposes individuals who actively practice discernment in their personal lives.

Second, *communal discernment requires group members to have at least a minimum level of trust in one another.* When we distrust others, we are not likely to be fully open to them. When we question their intentions, we listen critically. A low level of group trust suggests that members are not ready for communal discernment.

If we trust that everyone else is praying as hard as we are praying, then we will be more open to listen to their experiences and insights. When we believe that others want to know God's will as sincerely as we do, then we are less likely to dismiss what they share. If we believe that everyone is as open to the Spirit as we are, then we trust that the Spirit speaks through them as well as through us. In other words, faith in God's willingness to guide us through the Holy Spirit is matched by an equally sincere faith in one another.

Third, *participants cannot enter into communal discernment if they believe that they already know God's will.* If we do not renounce our preconceptions, prejudices, and prejudgments, then we are not honestly opening ourselves to God's Spirit. This is a question of facing, naming, and releasing our attachments—the suckerfish that becalm our soul's progress, the dust particles that clog the clock's gears. Communal discernment, like individual discernment, requires holy indifference.

Freedom from attachments means that participants are open to the possibility that any proposed option may be God's will. Consciously admitted uncertainty about the right answer is the only valid starting point for communal discernment. No one can really be entering into an honest search for God's will when he or she has a prejudgment, an attachment, or a predetermined conviction about what God's answer must be.

Fourth, *group members have a desire to do God's will no matter what it may be.* They are committed beforehand to living out the choice toward which the Holy Spirit moves them. Commitment to doing God's will comes before knowing what God concretely requires in a given situation. We cannot discover God's will when we plan to decide later whether or not we will actually do what the group discerns.

Fifth, *a group cannot engage in communal discernment unless members share a common identity grounded in their vision of ministry.* Members will talk at cross purposes when they lack a shared identity, the norm for all corporate choosing. Until a group has clearly settled upon its own identity, it cannot discern how to embody this identity. In some cases, the first corporate discernment will be the search for a common identity and calling. In other cases, an existing mission or vision statement provides a basis for shared identity.

Sixth, *participants will have developed a shared statement of the issue, problem, challenge, or concern.* Group members often argue over whose solution is best before they agree on a common statement of the problem. They end up debating their different solutions without asking whether they are working on the same problem. A common statement forces participants to work together to understand the whole picture. This shared activity helps them better understand their common interests before they focus on their differences.

Seventh, *all involved are aware of all the potential alternatives and are committed to becoming fully informed about them.* Group members agree to research and gather information about every possible alternative, not just their favorite one. They also agree to pool this common information so that everyone has the same knowledge and information. A group cannot maintain trust and openness when some members think that others are hiding, withholding, or manipulating information. Furthermore, a power imbalance is created when some people have information that others lack.

A Process for Communal Discernment

Before gathering for a communal discernment, group members will have already met several times to clarify their common identity, to generate all relevant options, and to inform themselves of the available information

about each alternative. During this phase, the practices of listening, skillful
discussion, and dialogue play a crucial role.

Steps in Communal Discernment

- Determine if group can engage in communal discernment.
- Complete prework on issue and alternatives. D₁f
- Engage in individual discernment. D₁f
- Gather with prayer.
- Set norms/review process.
- Participants share negative impulses or reasons. easy
- Break for individual reflection.
- Participants share positive impulses or reasons. easy
- Break for individual reflection.
- Open dialogue. easy
- Synthesis and resolution, referral to authority, or postponement.
- Closing prayer.

Individual Time for Discernment Prior to Meeting

Participants need sufficient time between the completion of the prework
and the communal discernment to discern individually what God intends for
them to do or to say. When they have this sufficient time, they will have individually explored their interior movements regarding each alternative. They
will have developed a list of advantages and disadvantages or engaged their
imagination in visualizing different possibilities. When the group meets for
communal discernment, they are gathering to share the fruit of their personal
discernment in a structured way. (See box above.)

Opening Prayer and Norm Setting

The facilitator opens the meeting with prayer, asking for the Spirit's
guidance and direction. He or she next reviews the stages of the communal
discernment. The facilitator then establishes norms for communal discernment. These include confidentiality, respect, acceptance of others, equal
sharing of dialogue time, permission to remain silent, and other norms that
group members may wish to include.

Stating Negative Responses to Each Alternative

The facilitator then invites each participant to state his or her negative
feelings, perceptions, or reasons for each possible alternative. These are the

individual discernments that each participant arrived at as he or she prayer-fully deliberated on the situation. The facilitator or a designated scribe writes these comments on newsprint, dry-erase board, or chalkboard.

Participants do not comment on what anyone says. The evidence shared is each person's experience of the Spirit's interior movement in his or her own life. Only the person speaking can vouch for this experience; it is not subject to debate or analysis. Because each participant is voicing his or her interior experiences, their comments will probably not be long speeches.

Silent Reflection

The group next breaks for a time of individual prayer and reflection. The facilitator invites participants to examine their conscience during this time. Two questions (below) guide this examination of conscience. Both probe for hidden attachments that may be distorting perceptions or compelling willful behavior.

- Where am I not free from hidden attachments with respect to the negative comments being made?
- What hidden attachments prevent me from listening openly to those speaking?

Stating Positive Responses

The group then reconvenes. Each participant tells his or her positive comments, feelings, or thoughts about each option. These are the fruit of each person's individual prayerful discernment on the evidence and situation. The scribe writes these comments on newsprint, dry-erase board, or chalkboard. Group members again do not analyze, discuss, or criticize these comments.

Silent Reflection

After all group members have told their positive reflections, participants again break for a time of prayer. The same questions guide an examination of conscience regarding hidden attachments:

- Where am I not free from hidden attachments with respect to the positive comments being made?
- What hidden attachments prevent me from listening openly to those speaking?

These four steps—stating negative responses, silent reflection, stating positive responses, and silent reflection again—are important to communal discernment, particularly stating negative responses first. This approach, on the surface, may appear counterproductive. Yet, curiously enough, it promotes unanimity. Participants are telling what they do not like about each alternative. They do not need to listen for their opponents' weak points because their opponents themselves are talking about the weaknesses of their positions.

Everyone can therefore listen without feeling that they must keep track of comments in order to present an opposing view. When group members tell all the negative responses and then all the positive ones, they feel less defensive.

This separation also allows participants to discharge their negative emotions first. They are thus ready for more positive work later in the meeting. Negative reasons always generate negative emotions, which in turn cause aggressive feelings. By getting these out of the way early in the communal discernment, people are free to listen more openly as the process unfolds.

Open Dialogue

When the group concludes its second time of silence (examination of conscience), participants are ready for an open dialogue. Members sift through the advantages and disadvantages of each alternative, drawing together the various threads of the earlier steps. Which positive assessments are really important? Which negative comments carry the most weight? Participants are not opponents trying to defeat their foes. They are, together, members of one community seeking to find God in a specific situation. As the conversation continues, it may gradually become clear which alternative best expresses God's intentions for this particular circumstance.

Voices that represent the marginalized or the underrepresented carry particular weight in discernment. God often speaks through the most unlikely people. When Samuel came to anoint Israel's new king in Bethlehem, he was certain that Jesse's son Eliab must be king. But God said to Samuel, "Do not look on his appearance or on the height of his stature, because I have rejected him; for the LORD does not see as mortals see; they look on the outward appearance, but the LORD looks on the heart" (1 Samuel 16:7). Although St. Benedict's *Rule* gives final authority to the abbot, Benedict instructs the abbot to listen carefully for marginalized voices. This emphasis on the least and the last, on the marginalized and the invisible, is part of God's calculated inefficiency. The whole is greater than the sum of the parts. The gifts of the Spirit are not equally distributed. So inclusive dialogue is crucial to discerning God's will.

Resolution, Postponement, or Referral

The facilitator may choose to test the group to determine if a choice is emerging. Each participant may be asked to say whether he or she stands inside or outside an emerging shared discernment.

No participant should feel compelled to agree with this emerging choice. God may call some individuals to stand against the group as a prophetic voice, representing a minority view. The goal of communal discernment is not unanimity.

On the other hand, just because one or two people remain uncomfortable with a particular choice does not mean that the group may not elect this intention. God may be using these individuals to represent an alternative position that keeps the whole group honest and fair. This minority, while assuming a prophetic role, should not adopt a self-righteous or obstructionist attitude. They are to maintain their position humbly, without dumping shame or guilt on others. As St. Benedict's *Rule* advises, this minority must not defend their views stubbornly or arrogantly.

If participants cannot agree on a common discernment of God's intentions, they should feel no pressure to reach a final decision. They may postpone their deliberation until another time. Members can engage in further personal reflection, prayer, and individual discernment before another meeting. When time or other external pressures demand an immediate resolution, the group may decide to settle the issue by a vote. They may also refer the question to some external authority, who makes the final determination on their behalf.

However the meeting ends, participants conclude with a time of prayer. They ask that God confirm their deliberation with a sense of unity and peace and that God grant them the strength to fulfill whatever God calls them to do.

Discernment and the Marks of Community

The practice of discernment allows small groups to remember that they are Christ-centered. Their common life is centered on God's intentions, not on their personal agendas and purposes.

Discernment also promotes healing and wholeness. Discernment requires that we plumb the depths of the self, uncovering the hidden desires and attachments that divide our hearts. As we confront these attachments, we experience healing and move toward wholeness.

Discernment fosters hospitality. The practice of discernment reminds us that we need others in order to see the whole of God's truth. In particular, we need to welcome the voices of the invisible, the marginal, and the forgotten ones. Discernment creates a free and open space where we may discover together God's truth.

The goal and purpose of Christian life is to live every moment in a graced awareness of God's intentions for our lives. God's intentions include our using all our gifts and graces for ministry. Discerning God's will encourages a group climate where people discover their gifts and live out their baptismal covenant faithfully in every life circumstance.

For Further Reflection

Do an inventory of the small groups in your congregation. Which groups might be potential settings for communal discernment? In which groups would an individual ask for group guidance?

What tools or resources do these groups currently have to help discern God's will? Where are preconditions lacking? Where are tools or skills lacking?

What next steps can you engage in to help these groups practice the forms of discernment most appropriate to their setting?

Chapter Seven

Body Building:
The Practice of Covenant Making

C ommunity satisfies two basic human needs: the need for relationship and the need for participation in purposes larger than ourselves. For the Hebrew people, covenant was the basis for community. Biblical covenants always include two or more parties who enter into a relationship for the sake of larger, shared purposes. Apart from covenant, there could be no community.

Covenant Making in the Bible

Biblical covenants sometimes involve two equal parties. Jacob and Laban establish a covenant for the sake of their families' future security (Genesis 31:43-55). This covenant defines their relationship and describes the common purposes to which they commit themselves.

Unequal partners may also establish covenant relationships. Kings make covenants with their vassals. God makes a covenant with Abraham and Sarah (Genesis 15). God's purpose of blessing humankind will be fulfilled through this special relationship. God institutes a covenant on Mount Sinai with a mixed band of former slaves, refugees, and migrant workers. Entering into this new relationship, Israel becomes a holy community existing for God's redemptive purposes. God's covenant with David formalizes a special relationship through which justice and righteousness will be established forever (Psalm 89).

Through covenant making, God creates the context where we experience the gift of community. Covenants establish a new quality of relationship. They also unite us around a shared purpose to which God calls us.

The New Testament frequently uses the word *partnership* (*koinonia*), rather than *covenant*, to express how we experience community at the intersection of relationship and purpose. Peter, James, and John were partners in a Galilean fishing business when Jesus invited them into a new partnership (Luke 5:1-12). Following Jesus, they would now fish for people. Because they entered into a new relationship with Jesus and one another, they contributed their time, status, labor, and material goods to a purpose larger than themselves. Partnership with Jesus involves a new focus of relationship and a new purpose greater than self. Such partnerships are the precondition for Christian community.

Paul frequently appealed to such partnerships in the gospel. He reminded Philemon that he was a partner with Paul in God's mission (Philemon 17). The Philippian church enjoyed a close relationship with Paul in which it supported his missionary work financially. This relationship advanced the shared purpose of spreading God's good news in Jesus Christ. Paul reminded the Philippians (Philippians 4:15-16) that no other community enjoyed such a partnership (*koinonia*) with him.

Paul's understanding of partnership underlay his gathering of the Jerusalem collection. As he explained it to the Romans, "For Macedonia and Achaia have been pleased to share their resources with the poor among the saints at Jerusalem. They were pleased to do this, and indeed they owe it to them; for if the Gentiles have come to share in their spiritual blessings, they ought also to be of service to them in material things" (Romans 15:26-27). The new covenant community in Jesus Christ emerges at the intersection of purpose and relationship.

Covenant Making in Small Groups

Small groups engage in covenant making. They develop norms that define how members relate to one another. They generate a vision of their common task that describes the larger purposes to which members commit themselves. Groups are more likely to experience the gift of community when members negotiate explicit covenants that articulate their norms and vision.

Many church groups develop vision statements. But they often fail to articulate their norms. Such groups are "playing with half a deck." Members are sometimes so committed to a group's goals that they endure its norms. Members of the Sunday school class suffer with gossip and sarcasm because they value learning about the Bible. The choir tolerates a temperamental director because members share a vision of their music as a way to glorify God.

Other church groups have neither goals nor norms. The young mothers' support group continues to meet, but its meetings have neither focus nor direction. Members drift in and out, adding to a sense of disconnection and discontinuity. No one is willing to terminate the group. No one knows how to help it regain a worthwhile vision.

Small groups cultivate Christian community when they make intentional covenants that specify norms and purposes. Through covenant making, members negotiate norms that reflect how they will relate to God and one another. Covenant making provides a process through which group members can develop a shared vision. This vision connects group members to one another and to God.

Group Norms

Norms are standards or procedures of group behavior. Norms are the assumptions held by group members about what is right or wrong, good or bad, appropriate or inappropriate, allowed or not allowed.

When a group does not have mutually shared norms, individual members operate on their own expectations of what is right or wrong, appropriate or inappropriate. They expect this group to function by the same rules as other groups in which they have participated. But such expectations may be incorrect. Conflict and poor interpersonal relationships result when small groups are unclear about their behavioral norms.

Cloydia works in a high-pressure environment where people often speak with brutal frankness. Since time is at a premium, her coworkers are abrupt and curt in meetings. When her congregation elected her to the church council, Cloydia brought these same expectations with her. She behaves in the council meeting just as she behaves at her telemarketing firm. As a result, Cloydia is alienating and angering other council members. Since the council lacks explicit norms, Cloydia does not realize that her behavior is inappropriate.

Healthy groups develop explicit norms. They do not permit members to operate on the basis of untested expectations that can sabotage group life. Healthy groups develop norms that
- use terms that describe behavior, not attitudes
- are brief and understandable
- are posted where everyone can see them at each meeting
- are reviewed and evaluated periodically
- are never used to incriminate or shame people

Covenant making involves the disciplines of listening, dialogue, and discernment. Developing group norms requires members to listen, to engage in dialogue around their differences, and to practice discernment. Group members can ask some of the following questions in building shared norms:

- How will we operate together?
- How will we run our meetings?
- How will we make decisions?
- How will we solve procedural problems that arise?
- How will we solve people problems that arise?
- What process will we use to prioritize our work?
- What will we do if we get off track?

Christian small groups also negotiate norms that describe how they will practice the means of grace:

- How will prayer and worship be incorporated into our group life?
- Who is responsible for planning and leading worship and prayer?
- How will we search the Scripture or engage in theological reflection?
- Who is responsible for planning and leading study and reflection?
- Will we agree to fast on the same day each week or month even if we are not meeting?
- Do we see Christian conferencing as integral to our gathering?

Members of St. James Church gather every January to organize their small groups. The Sunday-afternoon session begins with worship and a training session. The training session builds general skills in agenda setting, listening, or discernment. Members next break into their various small groups. They share expectations for how their group will operate and how members will treat one another. Each group develops an explicit statement of its norms that members can understand and accept. Groups post these norms at each meeting throughout the year. St. James's leadership team intentionally builds the congregation's capacity for covenant making. Such capacity building enhances the probability that small groups will discover the gift of Christian community.

Group Vision

Covenant making also encourages groups to develop a shared vision. Healthy groups have a vision for how members are contributing to something larger than themselves. One reason people share a vision is to feel connected to others in a significant undertaking.

Covenant making builds a shared vision that focuses people on purposes greater than themselves. Visions cannot be imposed. Leaders cannot force their own personal vision onto a group. They can, however, initiate processes that help members articulate a vision. They can offer criteria for discerning judgments about a vision. They can hold a mirror to the group's present vision, enabling members to assess the group's quality and adequacy.

At least three different visions interact in every group. Covenant community emerges at the intersection of these three visions. (See diagram below.)

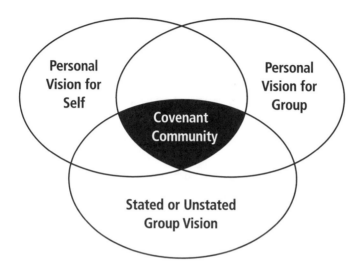

Each member comes with a personal vision for self. This personal vision for self expresses what one wants for oneself from participation in the group. Some people may join a learning or accountability group because they have a vision of themselves as growing in the faith. Others may participate in a service group because they envision themselves as continuing Jesus' ministry of healing and reconciliation.

Group members also come with a personal vision for the group. They have a vision for what they want the group to be or do. Bob envisions church meetings as gatherings that practice God's hospitality and inclusivity. He brings this personal vision for groups to Elm Street Church's board of trustees. As chairperson, Bob seeks to have the trustees embrace this same vision. Unfortunately, not all trustees share in Bob's personal vision for the group. His vision for the group sometimes puts him at odds with other trustees who have different personal visions.

Finally, all small groups have existing visions, stated or unstated. These visions represent the outcomes sought from the group's work and life.

The interaction between these three types of vision—personal vision for self, personal vision for the group, and the group's existing vision—explains much about group life. When dissonance exists between these three types of vision, groups experience either conflict or passivity.

Keiko's work trip to South Dakota inspired a personal vision of ministry to the poor and marginalized. She was delighted when a member of the nominations committee invited her to serve on her church's mission committee. After several meetings, Keiko discovered that the mission committee's unstated vision was limited to planning an annual mission dinner and coordinating the congregation's special offerings. Frustrated because she could not express her personal vision for self and for the group through the committee's existing vision, Keiko stopped attending meetings. She eventually found an outlet beyond the church for her personal vision.

Shared visions emerge from personal visions. Groups that are intent on building shared vision continually encourage members to share their personal visions for self and the group. They work to make the group's current stated or unstated goals explicit.

If members fail to state their own personal visions, they can only comply with someone else's vision. Visions take time to emerge. They are the byproducts of ongoing, intentional interaction between personal visions for self, personal visions for the group, and the group's present vision.

Visions arise from ongoing conversations where people feel free to express their dreams as well as to listen to other people's aspirations. Out of listening and dialogue, new insights into God's intended future emerge. Shared vision requires an openness and a willingness to entertain diverse ideas. From this diversity of voices and visions, members gradually discern a shared vision that transcends and expresses their personal visions.

No simple formula exists for creating a worthwhile vision. In fact, the more someone provides a clear, step-by-step outline for developing a vision, the less useful the outcome is likely to be. Genuine visions emerge from the disciplines of listening, dialogue, and discernment.

The practice of covenant making thus depends on the prior disciplines of listening, dialogue, and discernment. As we listen others into speech, we discover visions we never dreamed possible. Through dialogue we create shared meaning with others. When we faithfully seek God's will through discernment, shared vision emerges from unexpected places and unforeseen people.

Dissonance and Covenant Making

Setting norms and developing a vision appear straightforward enough. But they are not so simple. Group members harbor multiple expectations about appropriate norms. Multiple visions for self and for the group, as we have already noted, exist just below the surface of any group. The interaction between these components accounts for most conflict within small groups. At least three interactions play a crucial role.

First, *individuals themselves hold conflicting values and purposes*. Members of a support group may want to be nurtured and cared for, but they also fear being engulfed emotionally. Someone serving on an administrative group may have high achievement needs but may also want the approval of others. Members of a service group may want recognition but may also believe that they should be humble. The leader of a learning group may want to get something done but may also believe that Christians should always be kind and polite.

Second, *different individuals within a group hold conflicting expectations and visions*. Discussing these differences can be uncomfortable. Consequently, some individuals opt to keep their opinions to themselves and say nothing. They may pressure other members to do the same.

Group leaders can fear losing control if these differences become known and are discussed. They may choose to preempt conversations that bring these differences to the surface. Such leaders hold the group hostage when they appease or smooth over differences rather than allow the group to engage in listening, dialogue, skillful discussion, and discernment around its differences.

Third, *small groups exist within the congregation's larger framework of norms and vision*. These set parameters on what small groups may adopt as their norms and vision. For, example a congregation may encourage service groups to engage in helping people on a one-to-one basis but may not support efforts to address systemic injustice. In such cases a service group will quickly find itself at odds with the congregation if it engages in direct confrontation with elected officials over affordable housing policies.

These three reasons explain why small-group leaders need to give continuous attention to negotiating norms and vision. In addition to this ongoing attention, leaders also respond to particular needs that emerge at certain developmental moments in a group's lifespan.

Stages in Group Life and Covenant Making

All groups move through predictable stages. Covenant making occurs across a group's total lifespan, but covenant issues take different forms during each stage.

Inclusion

When a group is forming, it moves through an inclusion stage. Ambivalence and anxiety characterize this stage. Members are tentative, superficial, and polite. Questions are met with long periods of silence. Members are struggling with whether they wish to be included in the group. The key question is, Do I belong in this group?

Members do not have energy for large issues when they are deciding whether to invest their energy in the group. Groups dealing with inclusion issues therefore focus on short-term, immediate issues. They are incapable of addressing long-term concerns. Members focus the conversation on topics that they are comfortable with or that showcase their own knowledge and expertise. They hesitate to offer ideas, because they do not trust how other members will respond.

Groups can become stuck in the inclusion stage. Without clear norms and a compelling vision, a group drifts aimlessly. But leaders can help groups move through this inclusion stage. Groups dealing with inclusion issues are highly reliant on their leaders. Group leaders help members by modeling appropriate behaviors. They take the initiative in proposing tentative group norms. They can share their own personal vision for self and for the group, thus modeling how to share one's vision. They can also directly invite members to share their visions.

Leaders who personally affirm group members build up a fund of trust and confidence. They can name what is happening and encourage members to practice the disciplines of listening, dialogue, skillful discussion, and discernment. At a particularly difficult moment, they might say, "Some of us are understandably hesitant to jump into the conversation since we don't know one another well, but I think it is important to hear from everyone." Or they might interject into the conversation something like, "We are a new group, and it will take time for us to feel comfortable dealing with the differences between us. Let's focus on what we can accomplish now."

People depend on the designated leader to initiate group activity, to propose tentative norms, and to share his or her vision with the group. People's dependence during this stage does not mean they are weak or inadequate. Their dependence lies in the situation, not in themselves. Covenant making relies on the designated leader to model appropriate behaviors and values during this stage. When designated leaders fail to propose norms and set forth a compelling personal vision, groups find it difficult to move to the next stage of group development.

Some groups never mature. They remain chronically dependent on their designated leader. Chronic leader dependence extends the inclusion stage beyond its natural limits. It locks both leader and group into an unhealthy parent-child relationship. The group offers loyalty and admiration to its leader if things go well. If things do not go well, the group blames and punishes its leader.

Such groups prefer the comfort of being cared for and controlled. Their leaders have a need to be needed, all-wise, or all-controlling. They may fear the strong emotions and turbulence that erupt when members negotiate meaningful norms and visions. In many cases, they may lack the skills necessary to lead groups in the practice of covenant making. Such leaders enable irresponsible group behavior. In the process, they increase the likelihood of their own burnout and disillusionment.

Confrontation

The only way to move beyond chronic leader dependence is to submit to the risk and discomfort of the confrontation stage. As members come to know one another better, they become aware of their differences about vision and norms. Questions of power, dominance, and control move to the forefront. They ask questions like, How much influence will I have here? and, Over what parts of group life will I have influence? Members know they have entered the confrontation stage when opposition and criticism characterize group life. Negative comments are directed at specific individuals. Subgroups form. Turf and territoriality surface as important issues. Actions are taken to enhance individual status and importance.

Awareness of differing visions and norms dominates this stage of group life. Members struggle with how much control or influence they will have over the emerging vision and norms. Perhaps you have been in a group where people struggle over the precise wording of a motion, proposal, or vision statement. They go over the same seemingly insignificant word or sentence again and again. Beneath the surface, these people are struggling to put together power rather than just to get the wording right.

Leaders help groups advance through this stage by creating or reinforcing norms that prevent personal attacks or criticism. They open channels between members so that differences can be skillfully discussed. The practice of listening is crucial to covenant making at this point in a group's life. Once we feel listened to, we are usually more open to listening. Skillful discussion or dialogue allows differences to be transformed into an emerging vision that the whole group embraces.

Leaders must often propose ways for members to listen, have dialogue, and discern together. But the work of creating visions and norms belongs to the group, not the leader. During the inclusion stage, the leader took the initiative in proposing purposes and relationships that created a context for community. Now the initiative shifts from the leader to the group. The leader may propose ways for the whole group to work on purpose and relationship, but the leader can neither rescue the group nor control it. When leaders try to rescue or control, the group either becomes stuck in its conflicts or reverts to chronic leader dependence.

Leaders can help groups by naming what is happening: "We seem to be very irritable with one another. What's going on?" They can reinforce norms that prevent personal attacks: "We can make progress on this if we stay focused on the issue and do not hurt one another with personal criticism." They can remind the group of how the practices of listening, skillful discussion, and dialogue assist in the process of covenant making: "How can we listen to one another in ways that help us hear what God may be calling us to be or to do?"

Collaboration

The confrontation stage tests members' commitment to one another, their capacity to think creatively, and their ability to speak forthrightly and listen openly. Groups that successfully negotiate this stage then enter the collaboration stage. At this stage, group members are free to be themselves. They focus on the task at hand rather than on themselves or their differences. Service groups engage in service to God and others. Administrative groups undertake the decision making or problem solving assigned to them. Learning groups study the Bible. Members express support for one another as well as for the task. The group's norms and goals recede into the background. The group focuses on the task at hand.

Circumstances eventually thrust most groups back into issues of inclusion or confrontation, however. Changes in membership can trigger a reversion to either inclusion or confrontation. A change in the group's context—such as a crisis in the congregation or a change in leaders—can cause groups to revisit earlier struggles over norms and vision. Effective leaders and group members are alert to these changes. They help the group move through processes that review earlier struggles and integrate new circumstances into the group's life.

Covenant Making and the Gift of Community

Groups that grow in their capacity for covenant making simultaneously enhance their ability to receive the gift of community. On the other hand, groups that lack the commitment or skills to negotiate worthwhile norms and a shared vision have difficulty discerning community's presence.

Covenant making involves negotiating norms that include practicing the means of grace. Prayer, study, fasting, and other means of grace are often integrated into a group's norms.

Open covenants openly negotiated provide a hospitable environment for group members. Hostile environments are characterized by uncertainty over what is expected or how one is to act.

Covenants based upon the New Testament concept of partnership or *koinonia* remind everyone that all relationships have a new focus in Jesus Christ. God in Christ is the third partner in all partnerships in the gospel.

For Further Reflection

List in the first column on page 84 all your congregation's small groups. Identify in the second column each small group's developmental stage. List in the third column what tools, resources, or practices are needed to help this group move to the next stage in its covenant development.

Group	Developmental Stage	Tool, Resource, or Practice Needed

Chapter Eight

Standing in Need of Prayer:
The Practice of Praying and Reflecting Together

Pablo dropped into his chair breathless after taking the stair steps two at a time. He had left work early and driven through an hour of rush-hour traffic. A few minutes after 7:00 P.M., he arrived at the district ministry team meeting. A young man with a guitar was inviting everyone to join in a praise chorus.

For the next half hour, team members sang praise choruses and contemporary songs. The chairperson then introduced a meditative video to which everyone turned their attention. When the video ended, someone passed out a photocopy of a Scripture passage. Team members broke into small groups and discussed questions that linked the video to biblical images and themes. The ministry team finally moved into a consideration of upcoming district events, budget issues, and future planning a few minutes after 9:00 P.M.

Pablo was quietly smoldering in his chair. He did not object to prayer or song or Bible study. In fact, he thought worship and prayer should be part of the team's life and work. The team meeting should be an opportunity to experience ministry as well as to plan for ministry. It should open people to larger energies and connect them to God and one another. But somehow the balance between worship and work was wrong.

Pablo slipped quietly out of the room at 9:45 P.M. His carpool would leave the parking lot at 6:00 A.M. the next morning. He could stay no longer. A few other team members had already drifted away. The ministry team had finished only the second item on a rather long agenda.

Another team member joined Pablo in exiting the building. "It's one way to make sure pastors make all the decisions," he grumbled. "If they drag out the meeting until we laypeople finally leave because we have to get up and go to work tomorrow, then they can make whatever decisions they want."

Pablo was still complaining about the ministry team meeting as he carpooled to work the next morning. From the backseat of the van, Linda announced that she too had attended a church meeting the previous night. But her experience had been totally different. The chairperson had read a few paragraphs from a newspaper column as an opening meditation. The church board then plunged into a heated discussion of whether or not to remove the shrubs in front of the church. "There was nothing spiritual in that meeting," Linda exclaimed. "I could have been at any community or corporate meeting. Nothing we said or did identified us as a Christian group."

Sometimes we are so busy *planning for* the church that we forget to *be* the church. We separate the immediate content of our gatherings from the larger purposes and goals to which we are committed. Linda's church board was so immersed in its assigned duties that members forgot to experience the gift of Christian community.

At other times, we are so intent on being a community that we undermine the immediate purposes for which we have gathered. Pablo's district ministry team was determined to be a community of faith when it gathered. Yet the strategy for experiencing community frustrated the group's own intentions.

Balancing Worship and Work

The criticism that "nothing spiritual" happens in our meetings is most often leveled against administrative groups. Yet other small groups are open to the same criticism. A service group feeds the hungry without ever praying or reflecting together on their ministry. A learning group studies the Bible or a contemporary issue without praying together or connecting the text to their own personal struggles.

As small groups have become more sensitive to the criticism that "nothing spiritual" happens when they meet, leaders have experimented with ways to engage in worshipful work. Finding the proper balance is sometimes difficult. The practice of common prayer and reflection is more difficult than it initially appears. Pablo's district ministry team was so intent on making their work worshipful that they negated the very sense of community they sought to create. Linda's church council, on the other hand, was not sufficiently committed to being the church, even as members deliberated on the church's behalf.

The amount of time members spend engaged in prayer, song, or Bible study does not necessarily determine whether a small group is "spiritual." Pablo's district ministry team assumed that the more time they spent praying and singing, the more spiritual or worshipful their meeting. But some participants did not experience this outcome.

Contrary to Linda's observation, the prevalence of "God talk" does not alone ensure a worshipful or spiritual gathering. People can use the correct religious words and phrases even as they attack, control, and abuse others. In still other situations, people's interactions may be prayerful, meditative, and spiritual although no one explicitly invokes God talk.

The practice of praying together has to do more with quality than with quantity. The depth of our engagement with one another and God—not the prevalence of "spiritual" language—characterizes faith-forming Christian conferencing.

Designing Common Prayer and Reflection

Two dimensions of spiritual experience are present whenever small groups gather. These two dimensions are content and process. Content involves the explicit topic or issue discussed. Process encompasses how group members interact with one another and with God. The content may or may not be explicitly spiritual. In the same way, the group's processes may or may not have an explicitly religious character.

A small group's content is spiritual when members deal with specifically religious topics or spiritual matters. Talking about prayer or sacred texts, for example, is explicitly religious content. Talking about last month's heating bill or personnel problems on the church staff, on the other hand, is not religious content.

A group's process is spiritual when members interact in ways that are genuine, generous, and gracious. Process is spiritual when participants experience their interchanges as an opportunity for faith formation, for a deepening of their spiritual lives. In such moments, communication becomes communion. Process is not spiritual when participants are controlling, deceptive, manipulative, or indifferent. Such processes deform rather than transform our spirits.

Process and content can interact to create several possible combinations. (See chart on page 88.) A small group may experience neither process nor content as spiritual (low process, low content). Members of a support group come together to discuss problems they have with their children. The convener does not begin or end with prayer. No one mentions Scripture. In addition, participants are rude and judgmental toward one another.

	Low Process	High Process
High Content	High religious content Low religious process *Pablo's ministry team*	High religious content High religious process *Accountable discipleship group*
Low Content	Low religious content Low religious process *Linda's church council*	Low religious content High religious process *St. John's trustees*

Linda complained that her church council was not spiritual. She may have meant that none of the agenda's topics were explicitly religious, that she did not hear enough explicitly spiritual language, that no time was spent praying, studying the Bible, or reflecting together. She may also have meant that the heated discussion and adversarial environment did not promote Christian growth or faith formation. Neither content nor process was faith-forming.

A second group may find that the content of their conversation is spiritual but the process is not (high content, low process). Members of the Berean Sunday School Class gather each Sunday to study Scripture. But the teacher is a dominating, authoritarian figure. He allows no room for opinions other than his own. Interaction between class members is kept to a minimum because he lectures for fifty minutes.

Pablo's district ministry team spent excessive time on spiritual content, yet at least some participants did not experience it as a spiritual process. They instead felt manipulated and controlled. There is a lack of congruity between the small group's content and its process. Participants in the district ministry team and in the Berean Sunday School Class received mixed messages about the nature and meaning of Christian faith.

Still another group describes its process as having felt very spiritual although the topic or content was not particularly religious in nature (high process, low content). St. John Church's trustees gather quarterly to review building and property matters. The chairperson carefully prepares an opening time for reflection and prayer that sets the meeting's rather mundane agenda in the larger context of God's purpose and vision. Trustees leave feeling that they have accomplished their work and refreshed their spirits.

Communal practices such as listening, dialogue, discernment, covenant making, and hospitality are leverage points for a meeting's spiritual processes. Their presence or absence has a profound impact on whether members experience the meeting as an occasion for faith-formation. Even in the absence of explicit religious content, these practices can ensure that the gathering's processes form faith.

Finally, a group may experience both process and content as spiritual (high process, high content). An accountable discipleship group meets weekly for lunch at a downtown restaurant. Members discuss their spiritual struggles and pray for one another. What they say and what they do are congruent.

People responsible for planning small-group gatherings have a responsibility not just for content but for process. It is not enough merely to place something "spiritual" on the agenda. This alone will not ensure faith formation, even if substantial time is given to this item. Attention to the spiritual character of group processes is equally important. Indeed, participants may not experience specifically religious content as spiritual if the underlying processes are themselves unwholesome. What we do speaks so loudly that people cannot hear what we are saying.

The communal practice of praying together thus cannot be considered apart from other group disciplines such as listening, dialogue, discernment, and covenant making. Adding a large block of time to a gathering's agenda for prayer or Bible study does not ensure that the meeting will be an opportunity for faith formation. How participants engage in practices that open them to the gift of spiritual community is more critical than how many spiritual exercises are packed into opening devotions.

The chairperson of Mt. Pisgah's stewardship drive committee began one meeting by asking members to talk about a time when someone's generosity toward them made a difference in their lives. This discussion set the stage for the remaining agenda, which dealt with plans for the fall financial campaign. Some questions for reflection set the administrative group's "business" matters in another, faith-forming context. Administrative issues were then able to open participants to larger dynamics and energies related to character, value, and purpose.

The same process can occur in other small-group settings. A support group for mothers can begin with a brief Bible study or focused reflection question that establishes a context for the discussion that follows. A service group can engage in reflective practice, using its reflection time to make connections between members' service activities and their faith. Such reflection links faith with faithfulness.

While such study, prayer, or reflection may take significant time, it may actually save time by helping the group to be more focused, cohesive, and "in the flow" during the remainder of the session. On the other hand, common reflection, study, or prayer may be counterproductive when it takes too much time or seems disconnected from the group's remaining content.

Designing Prayer and Reflection With Small Groups

Small groups provide opportunities for more participative, intimate worship and prayer experiences. Too often we limit our creativity in designing such experiences. Small groups can expand and share the Spirit's presence in fresh, imaginative ways.

As you plan prayer and worship with small groups, balance verbal times with nonverbal times. Move between discussion and quiet meditation. Encourage members to dramatize or engage in physical movement, then follow these times with space for inward reflection.

Remember to call upon the gifts of other members. Involve several members in reading Scripture, playing music, dramatizing a parable, or performing a dramatic reading. Small groups allow an opportunity to involve everyone.

To prevent conversation from expanding beyond your time limits, adopt a "three sentence rule." Ask group members to tell their stories, feelings, prayer concerns, or insights in no more than three sentences.

Incorporate short musical responses into your prayer and worship. *The United Methodist Hymnal* has a variety of brief responses, such as Taizé chants, that group members can learn and easily remember. Such responses can spill over from one setting to another. They build a common basis for prayer and praise in various settings across the whole congregation.

Remember that the practice of common prayer and reflection does not always have to occur at the beginning of a gathering. It can be scattered throughout a group's meeting time in imaginative ways. One church council uses the sections of Wesley's Covenant Service (*The United Methodist Book of Worship*, page 291) to organize church council sessions. Agenda items are grouped under headings such as Praise, Thanksgiving, Confession, and Covenant Making. A brief prayer, hymn, or meditation frames the transitions between sections of the agenda. Rather than thinking of opening devotions as a structure or order to follow, imagine that it is an unfolding story or drama in which group members participate.

Service and support groups, in particular, offer great possibilities for reflective practice. A pattern for this practice is suggested in *Letting Go: Transforming Congregations for Ministry*, by Roy D. Phillips.[1] Following is a brief summary of the pattern.

1. A group member poses a single question on which group members will focus. For example, How can I respond when my teenager violates our family's rule about being home by midnight? Or, How can I better control my frustration when the child I am tutoring seems unable to grasp my instructions no matter how many times I repeat them?

2. Other members can ask clarifying questions that help them understand the situation or the issue.
3. Members then have twenty minutes to voice thoughts and feelings that arise within them in light of the presenting question. They may not offer advice to others; they may only tell their own thoughts and feelings. The presenter reflects what each speaker just said, ensuring that the intended message has been accurately received.
4. Once everyone has spoken, group members enter into five minutes of silence. Each member reflects on what he or she experienced during the twenty minutes of conversation. They can think about such questions as, What themes emerged? Where have I had similar experiences? Since these insights occur within each person rather than as a suggestion coming from someone else, participants are more likely to take them seriously and incorporate them into their daily lives.
5. Participants next take time to report any insights or connections they experienced during their silent reflection. These comments may or may not be related to the presenter's original question. They are instead a sharing of new learnings that may have come to group members.
6. Following another brief period of silence, participants are invited to contribute any faith-based insights or images (such as phrases, Bible verses, symbols, songs) that have arisen within them during the session. Where has God's Spirit stirred them during the session?

Small-group settings usually allow for greater movement and physical involvement. Members can stand in a prayer circle. They can gather around a bowl of water. As they touch the water and one another, members can tell of experiences of humble service. Standing or sitting around a loaf of bread, members can recount a recent time in which Christ fed them with the bread of life. The person holding the loaf of bread tells his or her experience then passes the loaf to the next person.

Some groups light a candle to remind them of Christ's presence during their gathering. The leader can bring the group's attention back to this candle at various points during the session to refocus or reorient the group.

Each Practice Deepens and Reinforces Other Practices

The practice of praying and reflecting together cannot be separated from the disciplines of listening, dialogue, and discernment. Transforming meetings into opportunities for faith formation is not just a matter of expanding the time spent studying or praying. It also involves the quality and depth of personal interaction between members.

Indeed, all these communal spiritual practices are interrelated. Each unfolds from the others. Each practice enfolds the other disciplines within it. Practicing one discipline prepares participants in small groups for the introduction of the others.

Some small groups may enter into these communal practices through the doorway of listening. But they will quickly discover themselves acquiring the disciplines of dialogue, discernment, covenant making, and prayerful reflection. For other groups, discernment may be their first exposure to communal practices. These groups will soon find themselves learning how to listen, to pray and reflect, or to make covenants with one another.

Since many small groups already follow some practice of common prayer and reflection, leaders may find this discipline the easiest place to introduce the concept of communal practice. It may provide a natural platform on which to build toward the other small-group practices.

In situations where small groups have become stuck in inadequate patterns of common prayer and reflection, the introduction of other disciplines such as listening or dialogue may open the group to new forms of prayer and shared reflection. In some cases, leaders may find it easier to begin at the level of faith-forming processes and then move toward introducing new approaches to faith-forming content. This is particularly so where small groups have become stuck in unhealthy patterns or have become conflicted.

Each practice brings its own unique gift to a small group. Each also contributes something toward a larger, more inclusive faith-forming dynamic that opens members to God's gracious gift of Christian community.

For Further Reflection

Reflect on several small groups in which you participate. Using the chart on page 93, write each small group's name in the quadrant that best categorizes it in terms of faith-forming content and faith-forming process.

What tools, resources, or experiences do these groups need in order to move to another part of the quadrangle?

Using some of the ideas in this chapter, design an ideal faith-forming gathering. What would need to happen for all small-group gatherings to have these characteristics?

Endnote

1 See *Letting Go: Transforming Congregations for Ministry*, by Roy D. Phillips (The Alban Institute, Inc., 1999); pages 128–129.

	Low Process	**High Process**
High Content		
Low Content		

Chapter Nine

Welcoming Strangers:
The Practice of Hospitality

I n Robert Wuthnow's study of small groups and America's search for com-
munity, *Sharing the Journey: Support Groups and America's New Quest for
Community*, he balances praise of small groups with a warning about their
dangers.[1] Small groups provide opportunities for people to grow as individuals.
They bring diverse people together and enhance a community's social capital.
But small groups also pose potential risks.

They tend toward exclusivity, squeezing out people who do not fit their
norms. They become places where only the like-minded feel comfortable.

Small groups can promote prejudice and stereotyping. Since congregations
usually organize small groups around common interests, most groups exhibit
homogeneity. Everyone has similar experiences or values. This homogeneity
can reinforce negative stereotypes about people who are different.

Small groups can so emphasize intimacy and acceptance that they smooth
over differences of opinion or experience. This tendency to suppress divergent
viewpoints is so common that researchers have named it *groupthink*.

Small groups can encourage a spirituality that feels good. Feeling close to
others replaces being challenged and transformed. Interpersonal intimacy
becomes the sole standard by which religious experiences are judged. According to the "gospel" of small groups, we are saved by interpersonal intimacy
rather than by grace.

Martino joined a team at Trinity Church that serves Tuesday lunches at a local homeless shelter. After a few visits he dropped out. On the surface, everyone was pleasant to Martino; yet he never felt comfortable. Most group members were young parents whose conversations revolved around their children. Martino was single, and the conversations made him feel like an outsider.

Tricia was excited when her pastor asked her to serve on St. John's long-range planning team. She came to the first meeting full of ideas and enthusiasm. Tricia and a few other team members quickly found themselves at odds with long-term leaders who held different opinions from theirs. Rather than deal with these differences, the chairperson smoothed over the conflict. Silencing these differences weakened the group. Tricia sat quietly through the next few meetings. She then "accidentally" scheduled other obligations on the same evenings as team meetings. Finally, she resigned.

John likes his Sunday school class. Members spend the first half-hour singing hymns and praise choruses. Members call out a favorite song and everyone joins in singing. The Bible study remains superficial, but the lesson is not important to most members. They come to sing their favorite hymns. John has recently begun to feel that the class encourages a feel-good spirituality. It avoids topics that spiritually challenge members. Members focus instead on familiar songs that give everyone a warm feeling and reinforce present piety.

Hospitality Offers Acceptance Without Demanding Conformity

Small groups that practice hospitality are less likely to display these negative behaviors. Hospitality means allowing strangers to remain different—even a bit foreign and challenging—while nonetheless offering acceptance. Hospitality reminds us to value the stranger as someone who already has a relationship with us. This relationship is rooted in our common humanity in Christ. It does not depend on interpersonal intimacy.

Hospitality Offers Acceptance

The demand for intimacy distorts and can eventually destroy the very basis for community. Ironically, the quest for intimacy—salvation by interpersonal warmth—drives people apart. They cling to each other. Interpersonal boundaries are blurred. Members try to hide what others might reject. Anxiety and emotional reactivity increase. Relationships become distorted, dishonest, and potentially self-destructive. An emotional tangle replaces the richness of community.

Hospitality means offering acceptance based on a common relationship in Jesus Christ. We remain clear about our distinctness from one another. We welcome strangers without demanding that they become just like us. Hospitality does not collapse boundaries between people. It respects and values differences. Our differences become a gift to celebrate, not a deficit to correct.

Hospitality Enriches Experience

Strangers represent new ideas and experiences. Strangers challenge us to widen our horizons. We resist strangers precisely because they represent the unknown, the new, the different. We feel uneasy around strangers because their presence opens us to change and transformation.

Welcoming strangers opens us to new possibilities. When we welcome strangers, they share unexpected gifts and blessings. John's Sunday school class prefers to spend time with familiar hymns and choruses. These songs are like old friends. The class resists entering the strange world of the Bible, where they might confront perspectives that challenge their comfortable lives.

Hospitality Embraces Differences

We feel invisible in inhospitable space. Even worse, we feel visible but on trial. Inhospitable settings exclude. They smooth over differences. They render invisible those who are different. Members must either hide aspects of the self or exit the group. Tricia felt that she was in inhospitable space. She and her opinions were visible but on trial. An old proverb says the hammer hits the nail that sticks up. Tricia felt pounded by the planning team because she did not conform. Martino, on the other hand, felt invisible. As a single adult, the conversation did not include him.

Hospitality means accepting strangers without attempting to make them into some version of who we already are. Hospitality creates a free and open space where people feel safe to discover the deepest truth about themselves and their world. The biblical practice of hospitality challenges us to judge a small group not by its interpersonal warmth or intimacy but by its acceptance and inclusion.

The Biblical Practice of Hospitality

"Do not neglect to show hospitality to strangers, for by doing that some have entertained angels without knowing it," the author of Hebrews proclaims (13:2). The practice of hospitality has deep roots in biblical faith. Abraham and Sarah encountered three strangers under the oaks of Mamre. When Abraham and Sarah extended hospitality, the strangers gave them an unexpected blessing. They announced that Sarah and Abraham would give birth to a child (Genesis 18). Lot and his family offered hospitality to unknown strangers who wandered into Sodom. These strangers revealed themselves to be angels and warned their hosts to flee the city. When we receive strangers, they come bearing unexpected gifts.

Hospitality involves unexpected role reversals. Hosts find themselves as guests. The one welcomed as a guest suddenly plays the role of host. The widow of Zarephath welcomed Elijah as a guest into her home, yet Elijah ultimately became the host who offered food and sustenance during a famine. The roles of guest and host were strangely reversed (1 Kings 17).

Jesus consistently offered God's hospitality to those who gathered around him. Strangers and the marginalized were welcomed at table fellowship. The excluded found a hospitable space in his presence. "Go out at once into the streets and lanes of the town and bring in the poor, the crippled, the blind, and the lame. . . . Compel people to come in, so that my house may be filled" (Luke 14:21, 23).

Jesus' ministry was full of unexpected role reversals. The powerful invited him into their homes as a guest, yet he became the host, breaking bread and offering the blessing. Two disciples on their way to Emmaus welcomed a stranger. When they invited him as a guest at table fellowship, he became the host, breaking the bread and offering the blessing. This stranger, they discovered, was the risen Christ hosting them, offering them the gift of heavenly manna (Luke 24).

Hospitality and Small Groups

Small groups practice hospitality when they monitor for patterns or processes that exclude. These dynamics are not usually intentional or overt. They are hidden, buried beneath the surface of group interactions and processes. Members of Martino's service group were not trying to make him feel like an outsider. They were probably puzzled and disappointed when he did not return. Periodic assessment and intentional reflection can help groups observe and address subtle patterns and processes that exclude.

Small groups practice hospitality when they anticipate and encourage unexpected role reversals. Leaders relinquish authority. Quiet members unexpectedly take the lead.

Tyrone was a member of Salem Church's Angels on Assignment, a group of men who volunteered to do small repairs for elderly people. Tyrone was a quiet, somewhat withdrawn worker. He regularly showed up and did whatever the team leader assigned. One Saturday, Angels on Assignment was repairing a sagging porch step. The project's designated leader was unsure how to proceed. Tyrone, who had recently made a similar repair to his own home, took the initiative in organizing the work. Rather than feeling threatened and resisting Tyrone's leadership, the leader took on a supportive role. Groups practice hospitality when they anticipate and encourage such role reversals. They know that these reversals bring blessings and release gifts for ministry.

Groups that practice hospitality do not have rigid patterns of leadership. They do not have pecking orders that rank and classify members. Inhospitable groups arrange people according to gradations of maturity or growth. The "more mature" are viewed as superior to novices. In hospitable space even the newest and least "mature" member can unexpectedly play the role of host, sharing a blessing with the "more mature."

A few years ago, I made a spiritual pilgrimage to a labyrinth (a pattern on the ground that one walks the path of as a spiritual discipline). The constant switchbacks and the winding path altered my perceptions. As I walked the labyrinth, I could not tell where I stood in relation to other pilgrims on the same path. I could not judge accurately if they were ahead of or behind me. Sometimes I felt that I was ahead of others, but I was actually far behind them. Gradually I lost track of who was ahead and who was behind. I simply rejoiced in our common journey and appreciated those moments when someone walked alongside me.

Among its other lessons, the labyrinth taught me that all the ways we rank and categorize people—above or below, mature or novice, ahead or behind—are illusions. We are all pilgrims on the same journey. We walk side by side. We cannot judge who is ahead and who is behind, who is close to God and who is far away. Hospitable space welcomes others as fellow pilgrims without needing to fit them into a pecking order. Only inhospitable space classifies, ranks, and judges.

Hospitality means that small groups do not use interpersonal closeness as a criterion for faithfulness. Intimacy and warmth are not the most important standards by which we judge a group. Warmth and intimacy may or may not happen, yet the group may still be faithful. Members of a service group may or may not develop interpersonal intimacy, but they can still grow as they offer one another acceptance and work side by side. Accountability groups are judged ultimately by how they foster faith formation, not by the degree of interpersonal warmth and closeness. Some administrative groups fall victim to *groupthink* because members smooth over differences in the name of Christian love.

Hospitality creates a free and open space where all people feel welcomed, safe, and accepted. While these qualities are similar to interpersonal categories of warmth and intimacy, they are not identical to them.

The Practice of Hospitality and Other Communal Disciplines

Hospitality, listening, dialogue, discernment, and other communal spiritual practices mutually reinforce one another. Hospitality creates a climate where listening occurs naturally and spontaneously. At the same time, listening itself engenders a hospitable environment. Dialogue means a willing engagement with another's perspective, no matter how strange or different it may appear. Dialogue thus produces a hospitable climate. Conversely, hospitality sets the context in which dialogue can occur. The two disciplines are intertwined and inseparable.

Discussion and debate characterize inhospitable groups. Most of the seven preconditions for discernment describe qualities conducive to hospitality. In a hospitable small group, we can discern the deepest truth about ourselves and our world.

Covenant making, likewise, fosters hospitality. Groups committed to hospitality pay careful attention to how members covenant with one another. When group norms and goals are open to a newcomer's inspection and negotiation, the group extends hospitality to strangers.

Hospitality takes different forms in the five types of small groups. Each group nonetheless embodies Jesus' welcoming of the stranger as it orders and sustains its common life. The practice of hospitality is integral to how Christian small groups witness to Jesus' ongoing presence in their own life and in the larger world.

Hospitality and the Marks of Community

Hospitality is both a mark of community and a means to receive the gift of community. Hospitality encourages unexpected role reversals. Leaders become followers; followers become leaders. Flexible roles and rotating leadership encourage Christian believers to discover their own gifts for ministry and to be equipped to live out their baptismal covenant. Hospitality reminds us that in welcoming the stranger we keep Christ, rather than our own prejudices and preferences, at the center. In welcoming the physical stranger, we learn to welcome the inner stranger—those parts of the self we have repressed, ignored, or refused to recognize. Hospitality thus promotes healing and wholeness.

For Further Reflection

Describe a group in which you felt unwelcomed, invisible, or excluded. What specific words, behaviors, or processes contributed to this feeling?

Describe a group in which you felt welcomed and included. What specific words, behaviors, or processes contributed to this feeling?

Compare the two lists you have created. How can these lists become criteria for assessing the hospitality of small groups in which you participate?

Hospitality offers acceptance without demanding interpersonal closeness. What does this look like at a practical level?

Endnote

1 See *Sharing the Journey: Support Groups and America's New Quest for Community*, by Robert Wuthnow (The Free Press, 1994).

Chapter Ten

Among You As One Who Serves:
The Practice of Leadership

Faithful leaders do not insist on stopping ministries with which they disagree. They do not demand that they have the last word. They do not regard leadership as a permanent entitlement, a possession, a symbol of status and domination. Their movement is not upward and outward. It is downward and inward.

The Journey Is Not Upward and Outward

The journey upward and outward is a cul-de-sac where everything curves back upon itself in self-centeredness and pride. Someone once described hell as a place where everyone is perpetually obsessed with his or her own dignity and advancement. Everyone nurses a grievance. Envy, self-importance, and resentment motivate people. When leaders see themselves as moving upward into positions over others, they have descended down to hell. Unfortunately, they usually drag their groups into the same pit.

A Babylonian creation myth describes how the god Marduk overcame chaos through violence. Marduk slayed the dragon Tiamat. He then split open Tiamat's body and created the world on her dead carcass. Marduk ascended to kingship on a foundation of violence and domination. According to this ancient myth, leaders bring order out of chaos through violence and control. Such ancient understandings continue to guide some contemporary leaders.

They believe they have power by disempowering others.

Jesus, who was undoubtedly familiar with the Babylonian creation myth, practiced another way of leading: "You know that among the Gentiles those whom they recognize as their rulers lord it over them, and their great ones are tyrants over them. But it is not so among you; but whoever wishes to become great among you must be your servant, and whoever wishes to be first among you must be slave of all. For the Son of Man came not to be served but to serve, and to give his life a ransom for many" (Mark 10:42-45).

Jesus led by serving rather than by dominating. He invited his followers to practice this same self-giving leadership. Today's small-group leaders undertake a journey that is downward and inward.

The Journey Inward

The inward journey begins when small-group leaders give special attention to their spiritual lives. This spiritual journey is what genuine Christian leadership is all about. Without it, leading may do more harm than good. Leaders disconnected from God are adrift and unfocused. They are severed from their real source of power. Cut off from an ever-growing relationship with God, leaders can focus only on their own agendas, desires, fears, or self-fulfillment.

Leaders may become so busy doing things for God that they neglect to spend time with God. This lack of a personal relationship with God remains unacknowledged, however, because the leader is always speaking of God and making reference to God. When this happens, leaders become "glittering images." In Susan Howatch's novel *Glittering Images*, religious leaders seem spiritual.[1] They charm and bedazzle. They quote Scripture, pray, preach powerful sermons, and administer the church's affairs. Yet beneath this glittering surface of religiosity, they have lost all touch with the reality of God in their lives. They hold to the outward form of godliness but lack its substance (2 Timothy 3:5).

In Acts 19:13-17, some itinerant exorcists attempted to drive out demons by invoking the name of Jesus. They called upon Jesus but did not personally know him. They took on the guise of spiritual authority but lacked its substance. The results were disastrous. The man whose evil spirits they were exorcizing attacked them: "Then the man with the evil spirit leaped on them, mastered them all, and so overpowered them that they fled out of the house naked and wounded" (Acts 19:13-16).

Spiritual disciplines are not a duty imposed on small-group leaders. They represent precious opportunities to nourish our deep hunger for God's love and grace. They are means of grace. Through faithfully attending to these means of grace, we nourish our relationship with the One who loves us into life and being. Christian leadership flows from the energy and power generated by this love relationship with God. For leadership to be faithful and focused, leaders center their attention on God rather than on themselves. Christian small-group leadership cannot exist apart from this ongoing, personal relationship with God in Christ.

Spiritual Disciplines as Means of Grace

Leaders can faithfully guide others in the faith only when they themselves practice spiritual disciplines. Leaders can too easily center their work upon their own wants and desires. Spiritual disciplines keep leaders focused on God and not their own needs. Practicing the means of grace reminds leaders that the fruit of the Spirit always takes precedence over the gifts of the Spirit (Galatians 5:22-26).

John Wesley, founder of the Methodist movement, divided personal spiritual disciplines into instituted means of grace and prudential means of grace. Instituted means of grace include acts of piety such as prayer; searching the Scriptures; worship, especially the sacrament of the Lord's Supper; fasting; and Christian conference or conversation. Most of these instituted means of grace contribute to personal holiness. Prudential means of grace describe acts of mercy and justice. Some acts of mercy are directed toward individuals. One might serve the poor and marginalized, for example. Acts of justice, on the other hand, involve disciplined attention to confronting underlying social injustices.

Practicing these means of grace constitutes the heart of Wesleyan spirituality. Wesley viewed these disciplines as essential for all Christians, but especially for Christian leaders. Without them, we lack the spiritual stamina to lead.

The Journey Downward

As we journey inward, we discover the heart of God within our own hearts. But this inward pilgrimage is also a journey downward. We confront the dark and hidden places of our souls. We come face-to-face with our inner demons, with our shadow self.

As we grow, all of us suppress portions of the self that do not fit how we want others to see us. But these parts of the self do not disappear. They become a shadow self that remains hidden below the surface of our awareness. The longer and more thoroughly we suppress this shadow, the more powerful and dangerous we make it.

Eventually, this shadow self breaks out of the prison to which we have consigned it. When it erupts, it can injure both us and those we lead. This shadow self compels us to meet our unacknowledged needs through the groups we lead. We can project this shadow self onto the group, distorting its dynamics and interactions. Rather than our serving the group, the group then exists to serve our unacknowledged needs and unconscious desires.

Facing Our Inner Shadows

One of the biggest shadows haunting many leaders is a profound insecurity about their own worth as people. This insecurity is hard to see. Leaders usually seem confident and in control. Yet confidence and control can mask a deep uncertainty about one's worth as a person.

If we are uncertain about our own worth, we may act in ways that undermine other people's self-worth. Michelle leads a support group at Elm Street Church. Participants learned quickly that Michelle is an expert on whatever topic they discuss. Michelle's verbose, controlling behavior has gradually silenced everyone in the group. Most participants dropped out long ago, unwilling to tolerate her need to dominate and control. Michelle deprives others of their self-worth so she can bolster her own.

When leaders doubt their own self-worth, they may operate from a stance of functional atheism. They lead as if everything depends on their hard work and effort. To prove their worth, they pile up one accomplishment after another. These leaders act as if they are saved by their works, not by grace.

Mike is well organized. No detail escapes his attention. Unfortunately, Mike believes that if anything important is to happen, he must make it happen. Mike cannot delegate, because he needs to claim everything as his personal achievement. As chairperson of the worship committee, he does all the work. Most members have dropped out. Why bother to come when they know Mike will do it all anyway? Mike's behavior disempowers others. It also denies the power and purposes of God. Mike has forgotten the meaning of sabbath: God continues to uphold the world even while we rest. Everything does not depend upon us. It ultimately depends upon God.

Another inner demon for some leaders is the fear of death. To let a group or idea die is to be reminded of their own mortality. Some leaders therefore invest enormous energy in keeping alive groups that should have died long ago.

Louvenia leads the women's Bible class at Good Shepherd Church. Although the group's membership has steadily declined for many years, Louvenia invests enormous energy in keeping it together. When others give up tasks, Louvenia absorbs them into her own responsibilities. She threatens and cajoles others to attend. She scolds those who have dropped out. Louvenia refuses to let the group die, although everyone else at Good Shepherd Church accepted its death years ago.

Leaders who fear death are reluctant to take risks, yet genuine leadership requires stepping out on God's promises. Fearing failure, such leaders settle for quietly managing their groups. Such quiet management feels safer than taking the risky steps to which God may be calling them.

Leaders who fear death hide mistakes. They distort information to protect themselves and others from negative feelings. Their fear induces defensiveness. Fearful people are suspicious. They act unilaterally. Consequently, they cannot learn from their experiences; so they inevitably make more mistakes.

As leaders practice the means of grace, they experience God's forgiveness and grace. They encounter God's redemptive love. They come to know the power of Christ's passion and resurrection. Strengthened by these gracious gifts of the Spirit, leaders acquire the courage to extend hospitality to the shadow self. They thus deprive their inner demons of their power. They no longer project their needs onto the group, manipulating it to serve their needs. They are free to serve rather than to be served by the groups they lead.

Leaders Need Small Groups, Too

This inward journey is difficult and dangerous. It is easier to spend time controlling group dynamics than dealing with our own souls. The complexities of group behavior and organizational dynamics are easily mastered compared with the intricacies of our inner worlds. Leading others can distract us from the more threatening and dangerous work of probing our souls.

For these reasons, the small-group leader's spiritual journey is personal. Nevertheless, it cannot be private. Leaders need spiritual companions who can share the journey with them. They need soul friends who travel alongside them. This journey is too difficult and dangerous to undertake alone.

Many contemporary congregations encourage or even require people leading small groups to meet together in accountable discipleship groups. Just as leaders "watch over in love" the members of their small groups, they need settings in which they receive the same loving oversight and support.

Such groups serve three purposes. First, leaders model for the whole congregation the importance of ongoing faith formation in small groups. Second, leaders are less likely to co-opt small groups to meet their own emotional needs when they have another setting where these needs are met.

Third, these groups help leaders remain accountable for their ongoing spiritual growth, lessening the likelihood that they will become "glittering images."

Systems Move in the Direction of Leaders' Behavior

In most organizational systems, the whole system moves in the direction of the leaders' behavior. When we want someone to change, we usually tell the person what is wrong and what they should do differently. This tactic does not usually work, so we threaten, we coerce, we shame and blame. What we fail to do is model the change ourselves. A world of difference exists between saying, "You should change," and saying, "Get ready. I am changing."

A congregation will change when its leaders change. As leaders model the importance of participating in small groups, other members will respond.

Meeting the Need for Appropriate Support

Like the singer of a popular song, many leaders are looking for love in the wrong places. Leaders require groups where they can meet their needs for acceptance, nurture, and inclusion in all the right ways and all the right places. Otherwise, they may seek to meet these needs in all the wrong places—in the small groups they lead.

All leaders have emotional needs for acceptance, inclusion, and nurture. They should meet these needs outside the groups where they provide leadership. Otherwise, leaders may fall into the trap of meeting their own needs through their small group. When this happens, leaders lose perspective. They cannot offer the leadership that their groups expect and need. The small group serves the leader, meeting his or her emotional needs. The leader is then unable to provide the servant leadership necessary for the group to fulfill its purposes.

Paulo had a high need to feel included, to be accepted. "All of us need to feel important. Most of the time we do not feel that way," he once told his pastor. Paulo brought this neediness into the church council. As chairperson, Paulo talked too much and dominated council discussions. These long monologues, intended to please and impress his listeners, kept the group's attention focused on him.

Connie, Paulo's pastor, suggested that he join a small group of other church leaders for breakfast and prayer twice each month. Within this group, Paulo was encouraged to practice personal spiritual disciplines that deepened his sense of God's love and grace. This group became a place where Paulo received spiritual mentoring and soul friendship. He met his needs for nurture, inclusion, and acceptance through the breakfast group, so he did not need to project them onto the church council.

Watching Over Small-Group Leaders in Love

Leaders need to give special attention to their spiritual journeys. Leaders disconnected from God are severed from their real source of power. Practicing the means of grace requires persistent and consistent attention. Yet such disciplined attention is not easy. It is almost impossible to sustain alone.

Who would leave on a vacation to a strange city without a map? When we are traveling to unknown places, we almost invariably turn to a guidebook or map. So, too, when we enter onto spiritual journeys, we require people who can show us the way, serve as mentors, act as guides. We need others to watch over us in love along our spiritual pilgrimage.

Christian discipleship is not about leaps of spiritual insight or moments of bliss. More often, it is a matter of holding on, sustaining our relationship with God amid temptations to turn aside to other pleasures or pursuits.

Leaders best sustain spiritual practices when they participate in small groups that help them remain accountable. The Book of Tobit (from the Apocrypha) tells how the archangel Raphael guides the young man Tobia to a life of love and safety. Raphael does so in the form of friendship. Only at the end does he reveal his true identity. Leaders need spiritual friends who can be companions on the inner way. In such settings, leaders offer one another accountability, direction, and support. These settings for small-group leaders are supportive but not invasive. They come together in ways that challenge growth without rendering judgment or giving advice.

Developing Emotional Intelligence

Small-group leaders who have journeyed inward and downward have emotional intelligence. Leadership is more than technical skill or intellectual prowess. Small groups deserve leaders who possess emotional intelligence. Daniel Goleman identifies several components to emotional intelligence.[2]

Leaders with emotional intelligence are self-aware. They recognize and understand moods, emotions, and drives in themselves and others. They know how their feelings affect their behavior and relationships. They know their strengths and their limitations. Sandy knows that she becomes anxious and nervous when faced with too many tasks or deadlines. She more easily loses patience with herself and others. When her pastor asked her to lead the team responsible for planning the congregation's holiday celebrations, she declined the invitation. Sandy recognized that she could not add another responsibility.

Leaders with emotional intelligence also know how to self-regulate. They control or redirect potentially disruptive impulses or moods. They think before acting on their impulses. Self-regulation helps leaders create an atmosphere of fairness and trust. Self-regulation contributes to integrity. Many of the bad things that happen in a group are due to poor impulse control: Mary cannot resist an opportunity to take advantage of a misstatement made by someone in her support group. Max blurts out a critical remark. Leon cannot help himself when he has an opportunity to reveal a confidence shared in his accountability group.

Small-group leaders who possess emotional intelligence are characterized by motivation. Motivated small-group leaders are optimistic. They believe that God is gracious—all the time. Even when things go badly, they trust in God's providence and guidance. They keep going even when they face setbacks and failures. They know that their worth is not measured by accomplishments but by God's mercy. Doing God's will rather than receiving people's praises motivates their ministries.

Another quality of effective small-group leaders is empathy. They understand the emotional and spiritual struggles of other people. When we are worried about our own worth and status, we lack the energy to pay attention to how others feel. When we are anxious and fearful about ourselves, we cannot focus on others' feelings. Leaders who have gone downward and inward, confronting their inner shadows and encountering God's loving grace, are less needy. They are less self-focused. Consequently, they can extend empathy to others around them.

Finally, leaders with emotional intelligence have social skill. Social skill is not the same thing as friendliness. Leaders with social skill help groups discover common ground where different people can meet and agree. They know that nothing important is done alone. They understand that ministry happens through groups of people.

Self-differentiated Leadership

Effective small-group leaders who have a loving, personal relationship with God, who have confronted their inner shadows, and who have expanded their capacity for emotional awareness are capable of offering self-differentiated leadership. Self-differentiation involves defining yourself while staying in touch with others. It means being responsive to others without becoming responsible for them. (See chart on page 111.)

Louvenia, driven by her fear of death, keeps her small group alive by overfunctioning for it. Michelle resists insights into herself as she seeks to meet her

Undifferentiated Leaders	Differentiated Leaders
Resist insights into themselves	Increase their self-awareness
Refuse to look at their own behavior	Look at how they are contributing to the situation
Blame others	Look at their own behavior
Smooth over differences	Value differences
Are coercive, manipulative, emotionally needy	Define themselves from within
Cut people off emotionally	Stay in touch even when they disagree with others
Overfunction to prove that they do not need others	Function for themselves; allow others to function for themselves
Do not learn from experiences; repeat the same pattern	Are self-reflective; learn from experience
React to people	Respond to people

own needs through dominating her support group. Paulo, unable to define himself from within, coerces and manipulates the church council into validating his worth. Small groups with undifferentiated leaders become a glob of glue in which everyone is stuck together.

Differentiated leaders, on the other hand, foster a small-group climate where participants can grow. These leaders know that their worth is grounded in God's grace rather than in their accomplishments. They embrace the entirety of their lives, even those parts they find unattractive or undesirable. They are clear about their personal boundaries, so they do not overfunction for the group. Even as they define themselves, they have the empathy and social skill to stay in touch. They possess reflective depth and mental equilibrium. Members of their small groups grow because they are growing, changing, and being transformed by God's love and grace.

For Further Reflection

What is your shadow self? In what ways might you be having the group serve you instead of offering it the servant leadership it needs?

How are you currently practicing the means of grace? Which disciplines do you have difficulty with? Why? What needs to happen for you to deepen your practice of the means of grace?

If you do not currently belong to a small group that provides accountability for your practice of leadership, how can you take the initiative in creating such a group? Who, in addition to your pastor, do you need to consult?

Which of the five qualities of emotional intelligence represent your growing edges? What steps can you take to grow in these areas?

Endnotes

1 See *Glittering Images*, by Susan Howatch (Alfred A. Knopf, Inc., 1987).

2 See *Emotional Intelligence*, by Daniel Goleman (Bantam Books, 1995), and *Working With Emotional Intelligence*, by Daniel Goleman (Bantam Books, 1998).